A SYSTEMS APPROACH TO RECREATION PROGRAMMING

A SYSTEMS APPROACH TO RECREATION PROGRAMMING

By
Frederick C. Patterson ED.D.
Central State University

WAVELAND
PRESS, INC.
Prospect Heights, Illinois

For information about this book, write or call:

Waveland Press, Inc.
P.O. Box 400
Prospect Heights, Illinois 60070
(708) 634-0081

Dedication
This text is dedicated to my family.
F.C.P.
1987

CONTENTS

Community Involvement Approaches. Planning
Procedures. Other Program-Planning Methods.
Delivery Strategies. Primary Strategies. The
Cafeteria Approach. Indigenous Development and
Interactive Discovery. The Systems Approach to
Recreation Programming. Summary. Endnotes.

PREFACE

The systems approach to recreation programming has been developed on the basis of four major assumptions. The first is that recreation is a basic human need; second, recreation and leisure pursuits are becoming increasingly more important aspects of people's lives; third, these opportunities and services are provided by organizations; and fourth, systems procedures can be used to plan, organize, produce, and deliver recreation and leisure programs for people, individually and collectively.

The first assumption is based upon an understanding that recreation behavior evolves from and affects all aspects of a person's being — the social, physical, emotional, intellectual, and spiritual self. It is considered an expression of the self and it involves a vast spectrum of human endeavors that inherently contribute to an individual's sense of personal satisfaction, pleasure, and growth.

The second assumption is that recreation and leisure experiences make a significant contribution to the quality of most North Americans' lives. Opportunities for recreation and leisure experiences have been expanding as rapidly as advancements in science and technology have provided for a higher standard of living and increased earning power and productivity have shortened the work week and the significance of work for many people. In contemporary society, recreation and leisure activities provide the individual with a time away from the complex demands of modern living and enable a person to experience the joys of living and self-expression. These activities provide for the satisfaction of a person's inner needs, and for many they have replaced work as a source of a person's identity. In the 1980s, recreation and leisure pursuits represent an important aspect of a person's daily life and a significant investment of time and money. Collectively, the frequency in which people engage in recreation and leisure pursuits and the money spent on these activities has created a substantial new dimension of our economy. Individually and collectively, people now expect to engage in a vast spectrum of personally rewarding recreation activities.

Third, recreation and leisure opportunities are provided by organizations. All such organizations, whether public, private, commercial, or voluntary, function as social systems. The formal organization of recreation and leisure services provides for the concentration of effort, the control of resources, and the equal distribution and enrichment of services.

The fourth assumption is that systems theory and procedures can be used to improve the efficiency and effectiveness of the program-planning process. Systems theory provides a method of analyzing an organization's purpose, identifying its resources, and interacting with and synthesizing the activities of its component parts into a unified whole capable of producing and providing recreation opportunities for people individually and collectively.

The systems approach to recreation programming is a planning process that enables programmers to concentrate on the provision of activities that are responsive to the needs, interests, and expectations of an agency's constituents. The planning process is a synthesis of systems theory and existing program-planning procedures, providing a more efficient and effective method of planning. It relies on the analysis of information and technical procedures to make decisions related to the use of resources to provide recreation activities for people. The systems approach is a synthesis of information and instructional, operational, and management systems procedures, which can be used to plan recreation programs for any group in any setting.

This text was developed to introduce the program-planning system to recreation professionals, and to provide students in professional preparation programs with an effective and efficient method of program planning. The process can be used to plan a single activity or a comprehensive program, with the assurance that the activities produced are responsive to the needs, interests, and expectations of the people to be served. The first chapter provides an overview of recreation, recreation demand, and the systems approach. Chapter 2 examines the principles of programming and chapter 3 reviews the various approaches to program planning. Chapters 4 through 11 examine and explain the specific processes involved in planning programs and activities. The planning process is designed to enable the programmer to discover recreation needs and to organize the resources necessary to produce responsive opportunities for people. Chapter 12 illustrates how the systems approach can be used to plan community, therapeutic, and commercial recreation activities and programs.

A partial list of activities is provided in the appendix to illustrate the scope of programming possibilities. The systems approach provides recreation programmers with a basic planning process that can be utilized for any planning purpose. It is based upon the concept that recreation programs should be responsive to people's needs and that recreation experiences should contribute to an individual's personal growth and development and to the quality of life in general.

RECREATION

Recreation programmers, from the beginnings of the recreation movement to the present, have planned activities for people. Initially, recreation activities were planned for children and youth and programs consisted of activities of general appeal which could be provided economically. The recreation movement gained nationwide acceptance and support in the twenty-five years following its inception. Subsequently, recreation and park services have become permanent and legitimate functions of the organizations that provide people of all ages and circumstances with opportunities to engage in a variety of recreation activities.

Recreation is now considered to be an experience, rather than an activity, and program planners now concentrate on planning a variety of recreation experiences. Effective programming requires a planner to consider people's needs, available resources, and the effects of recreation experiences on people. The systems approach to recreation programming is a planning and decision-making process that relies on the effective use of information related to people's needs, recreation experiences, and available resources to plan and provide appropriate activities. There are a number of interrelated and interdependent interactions inherent in the program-planning process that are characteristic of a systems function. A system is any entity or organization in which people interact to achieve a purpose. The purpose of a Park and Recreation Service System is, according to Murphy:

> The primary purpose of any recreation and leisure agency, whether it be public, private, or commercial, is to provide opportunities for people, individually and collectively, to enjoy leisure behavior.[1]

The systems approach to recreation programming is a synthesis of management, information, and instructional systems' theory and practice. It is a process that enables a programmer to plan effectively and implement recreation opportunities in response to an organization's goals, people's needs, and available resources. A prerequisite for effective program planning is an understanding of recreation, recreation activities, and their impact on people. This chapter will provide a brief overview of recreation, recreation demand, opportunities, and systems.

RECREATION DEFINED

Recreation was originally considered to be an activity and people have struggled with defining it for decades. In 1949, John Hutchinson defined recreation as "a worthwhile, socially acceptable leisure experience that provides an inherent satisfaction to the individual who voluntarily participates in an activity."[2] Subsequently, modern progress has promoted the expansion and extension of recreation opportunities, making them accessible to all people. Recreation has become a means of self-expression; an opportunity for self-discovery and self-actualization through intellectual pursuits and creative, cultural, physical, and social endeavors; and it is considered a basic human need. Recreation experiences affect all aspects of a person's being. Gray, after extensive research, gave a new definition of recreation from a psychological perspective which provides for a new understanding of recreation, its effect on people, and a new foundation for effective program planning. According to Gray:

> Recreation is an emotional condition within an individual human being that flows from a feeling of well-being and satisfaction. It is characterized by feelings of mastery, achievement, success, personal worth, and pleasure. It reinforces a positive self-image. Recreation is a response to esthetic experience, achievement of personal goals, or positive feedback from others. It is independent of activity, leisure, or social acceptance.[3]

This definition of recreation expands upon the activity concept that has influenced program planning and identifies the psychological, physical, social, and spiritual aspects of the experiences to be considered when planning a program. Gray accents the positive contributions that recreation experiences make to an individual's sense of well-being. He calls attention to the fact that recreation can be independent of activity, leisure, and social acceptance. Recreation, therefore, can be any activity in which people control their involvement and it can occur at any time and in any setting. This interpretation of recreation allows a programmer to consider a variety of activities that have inherent benefits as programmable activities. Recreation experiences are not essential to sustain human life, but in modern society they may be necessary for a person to have meaningful experiences.

RECREATION DEMAND

Recreation is an opportunity for people to be involved in personally rewarding and enjoyable experiences which enrich the quality of their lives. It is an opportunity for people to satisfy their needs and the collective behavior of people seeking recreation opportunities creates recreation demand. In this context recreation need is an acquired need, as recreation experiences enable a person to satisfy basic physical, social, and psychological needs. A basic need, such as the physiological need for activity, will compel an individual to engage in an activity. For example, this inherent need will motivate a person to play basketball. There are a variety of human needs satisfied by recreation experiences and recreation demand increases in relation to the intensity of these needs.

Contemporary society consists of conditions that create the need for recreation experiences and intensifies these needs. For example, people now enjoy a shorter work and school day and have more free time, greater earning power, and more discretionary income, all of which permit participation in recreation activities. Concurrently, our technically advanced, often impersonal and dehumanizing society creates conditions that increase pressure, stress, and tension, all of which are conditions generally relieved by recreation experiences.

Park and Recreation agencies have responded to people's needs and have provided for a variety of activity opportunities. These opportunities enable an individual to be at ease, to relax, to seek diversion, to enjoy the natural environment, and to experience the freedom inherent in recreation. The nature of recreation provides nearly everyone access to its rewards. However, there are personal conditions that generally exist before a person experiences recreation.

1. A person must have a need for recreation.
2. A person must have knowledge of, and access to, recreation opportunities.

3. A person must have some knowledge, skill, or potential for a successful experience prior to his or her participation or involvement.
4. A person must express interest and engage in recreation.

Individually and collectively, these conditions create recreation demand, which originates from a continuum of personal needs, situational demands, personal motivation, and opportunities. People now engage in a variety of creative, cultural, educational, outdoor, physical, social, and service activities which provide personal rewards and give programmers a means of determining recreation interests, patterns of participation, and actual demand for recreation. Recreation demand is inferred from an analysis of actual participation and expenditures for recreation equipment and services. The National Park Service, for example, has calculated that people participate in twenty-four different activities five or more times per year. A Scarborough Report, cited in the October 7, 1983 Fund Development and Resource Report, listed twenty-six activities in which adults participate during 10 to 78 percent of their spare time. In a special report, the August 10, 1981, *U.S. News and World Report* identified the twelve most popular recreation activities in total number of participants. The activities are, in descending order: swimming, bicycling, camping, fishing, bowling, boating, jogging/running, tennis, pool/billards, softball, table tennis, and roller-skating.[4] *U.S. News and World Report* provided an economic analysis of recreation and leisure spending in 1981 by compiling data from the A.C. Nielson Company, U.S. Department of Commerce, and other sources, which predicted that Americans would spend in excess of $300 billion annually for leisure, recreation, and contentment by 1985. Leisure spending, according to this report, has increased by 321 percent in the span of sixteen years, from $58 billion in 1965 to $244 billion in 1981.[5] This is clear evidence that recreation is a very desirable human experience. Recreation participation and leisure spending in 1981 is graphically displayed by Figure 1.1.

Further analysis of the annual reports published by park and recreation departments reveals that increasing numbers of people are engaging in a variety of activities. It is apparent from these analyses that recreation programs consist of activities which an individual generally cannot provide for himself or herself acting alone but can attain through collective group action. People have—and will continue to—support all types of recreation and leisure services. There are thousands of public, private, commercial, and voluntary organizations providing recreation services in response to people's needs and demands for opportunities.

America Plays—

Participants

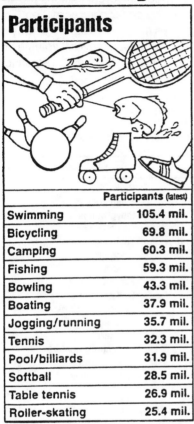

Participants (latest)	
Swimming	105.4 mil.
Bicycling	69.8 mil.
Camping	60.3 mil.
Fishing	59.3 mil.
Bowling	43.3 mil.
Boating	37.9 mil.
Jogging/running	35.7 mil.
Tennis	32.3 mil.
Pool/billiards	31.9 mil.
Softball	28.5 mil.
Table tennis	26.9 mil.
Roller-skating	25.4 mil.

Spenders

	Outlays (latest)
TV's, radios, records, musical instruments	$21,612 mil.
Wheel goods, durable toys, sports equipment, boats, pleasure aircraft	$15,446 mil.
Nondurable toys, sports supplies	$14,017 mil.
Magazines, newspapers, sheet music	$ 8,881 mil.
Books, maps	$ 6,962 mil.
Admissions to amusements, theater, opera	$ 6,424 mil.
Golf, bowling, sight-seeing, other fees	$ 6,150 mil.
Flowers, seeds, potted plants	$ 4,500 mil.
Radio, television repair	$ 3,658 mil.
Clubs, fraternal organizations	$ 2,295 mil.
Parimutuel net receipts	$ 1,898 mil.
Other	$14,581 mil.

USN&WR tables—Basic data: A.C. Nielsen Company; U.S. Dept. of Commerce; Daily Racing Form

FIGURE 1.1

Source: Reprinted from *U.S. News and World Report* issue of Aug. 10, 1981. Copyright 1981, U.S. News and World Report, Inc.

These organizations function within and are the components of a recreation and leisure-service delivery system.

In the United States and Canada, recreation and leisure-service delivery systems provide people with a variety of opportunities to engage in recreation and leisure behavior through organized programs and services. In this context, recreation programs enable an individual or a group to engage in recreation behavior using available facilities, which are the structures and areas in which recreation activity occurs. There is a cooperative relationship that exists between the organizations providing recreation activities and the people who engage in recreation. The providers of recreation and leisure services make an expanding array of opportunities available for people and it would take several volumes to list them all. The following table lists some of the basic recreation programs, services, and facilities presently available.

TABLE 1.1

Recreation Programs, Services, and Facilities

Programs	Services	Facilities
Arts and crafts	Information and	Parks
Performing arts	referral	Swim centers
Hobbies	Counseling	Playgrounds
Sports and games	Rental and loan	Gymnasiums
Outdoor recreation	of equipment and	Tennis and
Social recreation	facilities	racquetball
Volunteer services	Transportation,	courts
Instruction and	tours, and	Fitness centers
literary pursuits	excursions	Golf courses
	Concessions	Ice and roller rinks
		Ski areas
		Theaters
		Community centers
		Bowling and
		billiard centers

Recreation participants, who are consumers of the service, support the delivery system by engaging in planning activities and through their financial and other support. Consumer-participant support is dependent upon the provider's ability to produce relevant and responsive opportunities for people. The interdependent and interrelated cooperation that exists between the providers and the consumers of recreation is characteristic of a social systems operation. Recreation and leisure-service organizations are social systems, according to Ritter's definition. Ritter said, "A social system is organized human activity interacting to achieve a purpose."[6]

LEISURE-SERVICE DELIVERY SYSTEM

Leisure-service delivery systems and their independent and inter-related component organizations provide opportunities for people. The delivery system in any community may be composed of any one or a combination of all the public, private, commercial, and voluntary organizations involved in providing recreation services. Individually and collectively, these organizations function independently as management systems and cooperate collectively as a leisure-service delivery system. Hopeman[7] summarized the characteristics of a management system. They are listed with the characteristics of a recreation and leisure-service delivery system to illustrate the similarities of the two systems (Table 1.2).

TABLE 1.2

Comparison of Management and Leisure-Service Systems

Hopeman's Characteristics of a Management System	Characteristics of a Park and Recreation System
1. Systems have a purpose.	1. To provide recreation, park and leisure opportunities, services, and facilities.
2. Systems are special kinds of organizations and there are specialized functions within a system.	2. Including public, private, commercial, and voluntary organizations that provide community, therapeutic, and other recreation services.
3. The systems process consists of a series of *(a)* inputs, *(b)* processes when value is added to input, and *(c)* output that is related to achievement of the systems purpose.	3. Includes the input of recreation needs, interests, and demands and resources that are transformed into programs, services, and facilities through work transformation activities which include planning, organizing, staffing, directing, controlling, and distributing services.
4. The system exists in, relates to, and interacts with an external environment.	4. The delivery system exists in and interacts with participants, the social, economic, political, and physical environments in which it exists.
5. A system is itself a part of an even larger system.	5. The delivery system is composed of subsystem components that contribute to the achievement of the system's purpose in the community.
6. Evaluation and control are systematically achieved by a feedback process that promotes corrective action when corrections are needed to ensure that the system achieves its purpose.	6. Feedback is utilized to evaluate program efficiency and to ensure program compatibility with constituent needs, to control the use of resources, and to promote corrective action to achieve the system's purpose.

All organizations function as systems and are influenced by the environments in which they exist. Recreation and leisure-service systems exist to serve a constituency and they are influenced by the social, political, economic, and physical environments in which they exist. The primary differences between a management system and a recreation and leisure-service delivery system is in their purposes. Both systems utilize an input, output, and feedback process to transform information and resources into a product or a service. Their actual operations are more elaborate than the basic systems design illustrated by Figure 1.2.

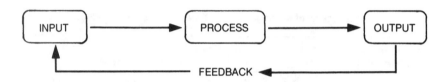

FIGURE 1.2 *Basic systems design.*

A recreation and leisure-service delivery system will use systems processes and procedures to coordinate its management functions and to promote and control interactions among its functional units or subsystems, such as parks, recreation centers, personnel, and program services. The systems are designed to acquire, analyze, and use information and resources to plan, organize, promote, and provide recreation opportunities for people. These opportunities include a broad range of programs, services, and areas and facilities. A recreation and leisure-service delivery system will acquire and use resources to provide the leadership, supplies, equipment, and areas and facilities necessary to promote responsive opportunities for people. The efficient use of resources and the effective planning of recreation opportunities require the use of a comprehensive planning and management process that ensures that an organization's actions are on-target or compatible with its goals, people's needs and interests, and within the scope of its resources.

THE SYSTEMS APPROACH TO RECREATION PROGRAMMING

Recreation program planning is the process of identifying people's needs and organizing the resources necessary to provide responsive recreation opportunities. The systems approach to recreation program-ming is a planning and decision-making process that enables a programmer to determine in advance the activities that will satisfy people's needs and how these activities can be organized. The planning and decision-making process involves the input of needs and resource information into a transformation process where systems goals, people's needs, and resources are analyzed by systematic decision-making procedures prior to the organization and output, that is, the production of relevant and responsive opportunities for people. It is an open and closed systems process and program planning consists of the following procedures.

1. Definition of the system's purpose.
2. Needs assessment; the identification and analysis of recreation needs and resources.
3. Development of program objectives; the identification and specifi-cation of the activities to be provided.
4. Activity and feasibility analysis; the decision-making process which determines the feasibility of conducting activities in relation to projected cost and benefits.
5. Operational planning; the detailed planning process in which resources are organized and allocated to produce specific recrea-tion opportunities for people, individually and collectively.
6. Promotion and implementation.
7. Feedback and continuous evaluation.

Each phase of the program-planning process involves interactions among a system's internal parts and with its external environments that ensure that outputs, programs, services, and facilities are compatible with people's needs and interests. The systems approach to recreation programming is a planning and decision-making process that enhances a programmer's or a planning group's ability to determine what is required to produce relevant and responsive recreation opportunities efficiently and effectively.

ENDNOTES

1. Murphy, J.F. (1975). Recreation and leisure services (p. 85). Dubuque, IA: W.C. Brown Company.
2. Hutchinson, J.L. (1949). Principles of recreation (p.2). New York: A.S. Barns and Company.
3. Gray, .D.E (1971, December 12). Recreation: An Interpretation (Summary of Research Findings). Long Beach, CA: California State University, Long Beach.

4. Our endless pursuit of happiness (1981, August 10). *U.S. News and World Report,* pp. 58-67.
5. Ibid.
6. Ritter, E.A. (1977). The balance of power for organizations, education planning services (p. 17). Greeley, CO: University of Northern Colorado.
7. Hopeman, R.J. (1969). Systems analysis and organizations management. Columbus, OH: Charles E. Merrill Publishing Company.

2

PRINCIPLES OF RECREATION PROGRAMMING

Recreation and leisure services represent a collective and coordinated effort to organize and provide opportunities for people to engage in recreation behavior. Recreation is a universal behavior, an expression of the self leading to the satisfaction of an individual's needs. Consequently, the scope of recreation activity is as broad and diverse as are individual differences. In fact, they are so broad that the agencies providing recreation services are constantly confronted with the question of whom to serve and what activities to provide and when, where, and how to provide them. Each of these questions represents a decision to be made by an organization committed to serving the recreation needs of people. These organizations are often confronted with demands for services that exceed their resources.

Management theory and practice dictate that organizations use goals and objectives, or principles, as the basis for making operational decisions. Goals, objectives, and principles represent an organization's understanding of human behavior and how the organization can best serve the needs of people.

The systems approach to recreation programming integrates an individual's and an organization's knowledge of human behavior with instructional and operational systems theory into a program-planning process. The planning process requires the programmer to determine the system's purpose before attempting to plan an activity or a program.

This is accomplished by examining a system's goals and objectives. The second phase of the systems approach to program planning is the needs assessment. To be successful, this process requires an understanding of recreation behavior and the behavioral sciences, which enhance a programmer's ability to relate human needs to organizational (system's) goals and objectives and recreation activity. This chapter presents an overview of goals, objectives, and the principles of recreation and aspects of the behavioral science that serve as the foundation for planning recreation activities.

GOALS AND OBJECTIVES

The systems approach to recreation programming concentrates on attaining an organization's goals and objectives by providing activity opportunities that are related to people's needs. This is a philosophical commitment to the foundations that have served as the basis for providing recreation and leisure services. In this context, a goal is an idealistic, visionary, long-range, challenging statement of purpose based upon needs which provide general directions for an organization's operations. Objectives are statements of intended action that are measurable within a given time and, when accomplished, move a system toward the attainment of a corresponding goal.

The programmer's planning effort is guided by a system's goals and objectives as he or she strives to plan, organize, and provide responsive recreation activities for people, individually and collectively. Concurrently, a programmer is continuously confronted by change which occurs in the social, political, economic, and other environments that affect people's needs and a system's operations. Additional issues, such as a maturing population, changing family structure, changes in workplaces and schedules, population migration, political philosophies, and the natural environment also affect people's needs. It is well documented that a change in any one aspect of a system's environment will produce a corresponding change in its other environments and affect a system's operational effectiveness. Considering the rate at which change is occurring in modern society, there is a clear mandate for a reassessment of the philosophical approach to recreation programming. David E. Gray, one of the futuristic thinkers of the recreation movement, has suggested that "Our traditional definitions of recreation have not advanced our understandings of it. For thirty or forty years or more the park and recreation movement has been deluded by a false perception of recreation."[1]

Gold[2], having considered the traditional concepts of recreation and the effects of change, has called for a new philosophical approach to program planning which requires an unparalleled sense of urgency, innovation, and professional sophistication. The new perspective that is influencing the development, delivery, and distribution of recreation and leisure services is based upon the holistic perspective, which eliminates the dichotomy between work and leisure. This perspective provides a foundation for reviewing and revising program goals and objectives and for planning individually responsive programs for people. The principles, policies, and procedures that guide an organization's programming efforts are likewise being reviewed and revised in relation to our new understanding of recreation and the changes that are occurring in society.

The psychological perspective of recreation, as advocated by Gray in chapter 1, and the holistic philosophical perspective of recreation, enable a programmer to effectively respond to change while planning more individually responsive programs for people. The system's approach to recreation programming requires the planner to determine the system's purpose, which is accomplished by examining an organization's goals and objectives. The goals and objectives of the Park and Recreation Department in San Jose, California, are reproduced here to illustrate the relationship between goals and objectives.

City of San Jose, California
Parks and Recreation Department
Goals and Objectives[3]

I. STATEMENT OF DEPARTMENT PURPOSE

Provide public recreation services of a significant nature and acquire, preserve, and improve park lands and environmental amenities so as to make leisure and the environment meaningful and worthwhile influences on the way of life of the citizens of San Jose.

II. MAJOR GOALS OF THE DEPARTMENT

A. PROVIDE MEANINGFUL RECREATION OPPORTUNITIES TO MEET LEISURE NEEDS OF ALL CITIZENS.

OBJECTIVES

1. Provide readily accessible parks, playgrounds, and community recreation centers to effectively service all portions of the city.

2. Utilize constant community involvement in recreation programming to provide the basis for administrative and staff direction in serving changing leisure needs.

3. Assist individuals and groups toward effective use of their own resources for satisfying their special leisure interests.

4. Interpret to the community the value and opportunities of available recreation services for meeting leisure needs.

5. Organize and conduct special recreation programs which contribute to ethnic identity and pride.

B. IDENTIFY, ACQUIRE, IMPROVE, AND PROTECT PARK AREAS OF RECREATION, HISTORIC, AND ENVIRONMENTAL IMPORTANCE.

OBJECTIVES

1. Maintain through community involvement a continuously reviewed master plan and a capital improvement program for parkland acquisition and development.

2. Preserve and enhance environmental and historical areas of a significant nature.

3. Take a cooperative and responsible role in encouraging and guiding future county and state regional park development important to our community.

4. Strive for quality maintenance and upkeep of all park areas and recreation facilities.

5. Support, initiate, and achieve city beautification activities including a positive street tree program to provide for a more attractive and livable environment.

6. Develop special recreation facilities and park areas which contribute in a maximum way to a community sense of identification and pride.

C. OBTAIN MAXIMUM PARK AND RECREATION USE OF ALL COMMUNITY RESOURCES.

   OBJECTIVES

   1. Work with all levels of government, other public juris-dictions (school districts, Flood Control Districts), and agencies in developing maximum public use of existing and potential open space and recreation areas.

   2. Encourage development of commercial recreation enter-prises compatible with meeting leisure needs of the community.

   3. Cooperate with quasi-public community service agencies on programs of mutual interests and concern.

D. ASSIST COMMUNITY SERVICES THAT ARE VITAL IN SERVING TOTAL HUMAN NEEDS.

   OBJECTIVES

   1. Be aware of community programs specifically designed for development of human resources and cooperate with those programs whenever possible.

   2. Refer individuals to special services where needs are identified.

E. ENCOURAGE CONTINUOUS BROAD CITIZEN PARTICIPATION IN ALL ASPECTS OF PARK AND RECREATION OPERATIONS.

   OBJECTIVES

   1. Include neighborhood and community participation in the planning development of park and recreation areas.

   2. Recruit, train, and utilize volunteer leadership in recreation programs.

   3. Utilize advisory boards in the organization of neighborhood recreation programs.

   4. Encourage citizen involvement and democratic procedures in the conduct of community recreation activities.

San Jose's goals and corresponding objectives are characteristic of progressive park and recreation departments throughout the country. Every park and recreation organization's operations are guided by similar goals and objectives and each organization and community should develop its own statement of purpose and intent. The effectiveness and efficiency of a recreation and park delivery system is determined by using goals and objectives as the criteria for measuring its progress toward meeting its constituents' needs and interests.

By concentrating on goals and objectives and by establishing a clear purpose for each activity offered, the systems approach to recreation programming provides for more accountability in the development of activities.

PRINCIPLES OF RECREATION

Principles are the guidelines that enable an individual or an organization to attain its goals and objectives. They are general laws or truths based upon available fact, opinions, and authority that serve as guidelines for planning and conducting recreation activities and programs, and providing opportunities for people to engage in recreation behaviors. The scope and dimensions of available recreation opportunities require that organizations reevaluate the principles used as basic guides for action.

The principles of recreation programming, suggested by authorities, have generally been compatible with the new perspective of recreation. A review of the literature reveals that Butler[4] listed thirty principles of program planning; Danford and Shirley[5] twelve; Hutchinson[6] six; and Kraus[7] fifteen. Tillman[8] suggested that "programs should be planned as a group or individual endeavor," and listed forty-one guides for action.

Seven principles for using the systems approach to recreation programming have been synthesized from the literature, programming manuals, and research. They are as follows:

I. Recreation leadership should be provided to plan, develop, and conduct activities and programs.

Leadership is the essential element required to successfully carry out the planned activities of any group or organization. Hersey and Blanchard defined leadership as "the process of influencing the activities of an individual or a group in effort toward goal achievement in any given situation."[9]

a. Leadership is, therefore, the process of identifying human needs for recreation, establishing goals and objectives (plans), identifying resources, and organizing these resources to produce recreation opportunities for people. The process is one of carefully planning, organizing, controlling, and promoting interactions among people and between people and their environments.

b. Leadership involves human relations, awareness and sensitivity, skills, knowledge, and the ability to motivate people, groups, and organizations toward the attainment of the mutual goals of all concerned.

c. Leadership is an art and a science. The art includes establishing interpersonal relations based upon mutual understanding, trust, and influence. Successful leadership is dependent upon establishing effective communications with all involved in the leadership situation. The science of leadership involves a systematic approach to the dissemination of information, decision making, problem solving, organizing, and controlling resources and recreation environments, and motivating individuals who willingly engage in a given activity.

d. The leader (recreation specialist) brings to the program planning and delivery system technical skills, the ability to use his or her knowledge in the performance of duties and responsibilities, human relations skills, and the ability to understand his or her role in relation to a given situation.

e. Leadership strives to improve the quality of recreation experiences by planning with and for people and then organizing planned activities and experiences that contribute to human development.

Leadership is essential for organizing and directing the individual and collective efforts of people.

II. Recreation programs should be planned to provide opportunities for the individual.

A broad array of recreation and leisure opportunities should be planned with and for the individual to meet his or her needs, interests, expectations, and abilities. The individual should be afforded an opportunity to select from a variety of activities that satisfy his or her recreation needs and interests.

a. Individualized (personal) planning is initiated to promote individual involvement in recreation and leisure programs. The individual is to be afforded a variety of opportunities for social, physical, cultural, outdoor, service, and other types of recreation involvement.

b. Opportunities should be available throughout the entire service system for people of all ages, both sexes, all racial and ethnic groups, and special populations without reservations.

Note: Activities that may be inappropriate for certain individuals because of their age, ability level, the risk involved, and/or legal liability should be restricted. Nevertheless, appropriate activities should be provided for all who wish to participate on a continuous basis.

Everyone, minority groups, special-populations members, and the skilled and unskilled should have continuous access to recreation opportunities.

c. The opportunities provided should span a comprehensive list of seasonally feasible activities; a person should be able to pick and choose from an array of challenging, interesting, and rewarding activities.

d. The program planned should include opportunities for involvement in (1) direct services, (2) enabling services, and (3) outreach programs. Recreation programs are for people individually and collectively and should be based on the needs, interests, expectations, abilities, experiences, customs, traditions, and values of people.

e. Opportunities provided by an agency should be related to the interests, needs, and abilities of people rather than an individual's or a group's disabilities or limitations. This is especially important when the disabled are involved in the program. The leader or programmer should accent the positive attributes of all persons and groups, and any limitations imposed should be for safety and risk-management purposes.

f. Individual involvement and input into the program-planning process are now expected and necessary to ensure that resources are used to meet the needs, interests, and desires of people. Provisions for participation in the planning process should allow for direct and reactionary involvement.

  1. Direct participation involves serving on a program planning or advisory committee.
  1. Reactionary involvement denotes participation by returning interests inventories or survey forms, or pre-registering as a participant in a planned activity.

In either case, the programmer is assured that the planned activities are responsive to the needs of people or members of their families, friends, and their associates.

III. Recreation programs should contribute to and enhance personal development.

Recreation behavior should be encouraged in all phases of human development, and programs should promote personal experiences in physical, social, cultural, creative, and other endeavors. Individual differences must be recognized in the planning process and provisions made for the progressive development of human interests, skills, and abilities. The development of an individual's potential for self-determination, appreciation, and self-fulfillment is a primary goal of recreation and leisure services.

a. Recreation programs begin with people as they are, at their level, and strive to improve the quality of their lives without superimposing a set of expectations or values.

b. Recreation programmers must recognize the unique racial and ethnic composition of our multicultured society and provide opportunities to enhance the preservation of the nation's diverse cultural heritage. Program planning with respect for the unique attributes of racial and ethnic groups and their customs and traditions achieves the objective of not superimposing a set of values or expectations on an individual or group.

IV. Recreation opportunities should be planned to make maximum use of available human and physical resources.

Planned, coordinated, and cooperative effort should be made to utilize available resources (human, fiscal, man-made, and natural) to provide for a comprehensive array of recreation opportunities. All public, private, commercial, and voluntary recreation and leisure services should be accounted for and considered in the program-planning process. Cooperation and coordinated efforts to use available resources by all recreation and leisure-service organizations is the key to comprehensive programming. Such efforts identify duplication of effort; duplicated programs should be avoided and, when practical, the resources used by one agency to duplicate the programs of another should be used to provide additional opportunities for people, if one or the other agency has the resources to implement new programs.

a. Professional and volunteer staff personnel are the human resources that make provisions and perform the tasks and duties necessary to provide recreation and leisure services. All personnel must take the responsibility of providing prudent and responsible leadership in supervising areas and facilities, and directing recreation activities, thus ensuring equal access and opportunity for all participants.

b. Professional staff personnel must assume responsibility for the prudent and responsible use of fiscal resources, while providing the most economically feasible array of recreation opportunities.

c. The same principle applies to the use of man-made and natural resources. Within the scope of available resources, all recreation areas and facilities, equipment and apparatus, and other amenities must be provided and maintained so that all participants have access to them.

d. Opportunities for cooperative interagency or synergetic programming should be investigated as a method of obtaining additional resources for the conduct of program and services. Private-interest groups, businesses, foundations, gift catalogs, and grants are sources of additional financial resources and should be continuously monitored to ensure that no potential resource for enhancing recreation and leisure services is overlooked or untapped.

e. Volunteers represent a human resource of unlimited potential and should be used in every aspect of an organization's operations. They are resources for extending and expanding existing recreation and leisure services.

V. Natural areas: the outdoors should be planned and conserved for a variety of recreation purposes.

Outdoor areas and facilities should be planned, acquired, and developed to enable the pursuit of a variety of outdoor recreation opportunities. Areas should be developed and maintained for maximum feasible use, while care is taken not to disturb the ecological balance of natural areas, especially those inhabited by endangered species. The whole programming effort should be committed to the preservation and conservation of the natural environment while encouraging maximum feasible participation in outdoor recreation pursuits.

Facilities for outdoor recreation should be planned and developed to complement existing land-use policies and community development plans. Multiple use of available open space for recreation and other uses is encouraged when feasible and practical.

VI. A recreation program should be subject to continuous evaluation.

The effects and benefits of recreation and leisure experience, whether occurring directly or indirectly as a result of an organization's or a person's intervention, should be evaluated in relation to the goals and objectives of the agency providing those services. In addition to an organization's goals and objectives, the evaluation process should include, but not be limited to, a consideration of the following.

a. The programs should be evaluated in relation to their effectiveness in meeting individual and group needs, the social interactions they promote, and the attitudes and values manifested by participants before, during, and after recreation experiences.
b. The evaluation process should reveal that the organization is actually progressing toward the attainment of established organizational goals and objectives.
c. The process should ensure that the leadership and facilities provided are appropriate for the individuals involved and for those not involved in the planned program.
d. Program evaluation serves to ensure that proper balance and diversity are maintained in the activity offerings of an organization.

The evaluation process should be systematically conducted, providing professional personnel and the general public an opportunity to discover and interpret how effective the organization is in relation to its stated purpose, and how it can improve.

VII. Alternative plans for each planned activity or event in a program should be developed.

The planning of directed or any other type of recreation or leisure activity involves anticipating the unexpected. Plans should be developed for alternative courses of action or activities in the event of inclement weather, schedule conflicts, or other unforeseen events. Alternative plans allow for maximum feasible use of available resources in providing for the substitution of activities or events when regular activities cannot be provided.

a. Planning for the unexpected allows for a minimum of delay in implementing alternative plans when a regular activity is unexpectedly interrupted. Considering the broad array of factors and variables that influence recreation and leisure behavior, maximum flexibility in program planning enhances the development of primary and alternative program plans.
b. Flexibility in planning means that planned activities can be modified or changed to accommodate foreseeable and unforeseeable events with a minimum delay in the delivery of services.

The principles of recreation programming suggested are for using the systems approach to recreation programming and are a synthesis of literary works of many experienced authors. Recreation can be considered a spontaneous expression of the self and, although spontaneous, it generally represents a rational choice. It is the individual who makes the decision to be involved in a recreation activity and he or she must have some knowledge of existing opportunities prior to becoming involved.

There is a final principle of programming to be considered. A prerequisite for effective programming is promotion. Recreation activities and programs should be promoted in such a manner that they will attract both participants and nonparticipants to the recreation place, and conducted so that participants will return again and again in anticipation of the positive experiences, the expansion of their interests, and the enrichment of their lives, which are all a result of recreation behavior.

THE BEHAVIORAL SCIENCES: FOUNDATIONS FOR PROGRAM PLANNING

Recreation and leisure research and the social and behavioral sciences, psychology, political science, sociology, and management science have provided new insights into understanding the recreation experience. The new understandings of recreation and leisure provided by the behavioral sciences have enabled recreation programmers to adopt and use holistic and humanistic goals and objectives as a basis for planning. Recreation and leisure-service personnel are now required to have a broad understanding of human behavior and how recreation experiences affect the quality of life.

The holistic concept of recreation considers it to be a vital part of daily life. Gray concluded that recreation serves to improve awareness, ". . . understandings, stimulates appreciations, develops personal powers, and enlarges the source of personal enjoyment. It promotes individual fulfillment, encourages self-discovery, and gives meaning to life."[10] The holistic perspective suggests that every human endeavor has the potential for positive experience, which is a major attribute of the recreation experience.

Individuals and organizations accepting the premise that recreation is a basic human need and that it contributes to all aspects of human development facilitate a programmer's ability to promote human interactions, self-discovery, and human development through planned activity. The behavioral sciences provide for an understanding of the impact that recreation has on human behavior; therefore, an understanding of psychology, sociology, and the physiological aspect of human behavior provide a foundation for understanding recreation behavior and for planning relevant and responsive recreation programs.

There are several approaches to the study of human behavior. The following summary of human development and motivational theory, psychological needs, and recreation behaviors is viewed as the behavioral foundation for developing recreation and leisure-service goals, objectives, principles, and programs.

HUMAN DEVELOPMENT

Developmental theory represents the integration of biophysical, psychological, and social concepts of behavior. Behavioral scientists have observed that some human needs appear to have greater intensity than others during different periods of life. Developmental theories such as Erikson's[11] support this perspective (Table 2.1).

TABLE 2.1

Erikson's Stages of Human Development

Stages	Characteristics
Infancy	Basic trust versus mistrust
Early childhood	Autonomy versus shame and doubt
Play age	Initiative versus guilt
School age	Industry versus inferiority
Adolescence	Identify versus confusion
Adulthood	Generality versus stagnation
Maturity	Integrity versus despair

In each stage, the individual develops patterns of behavior that are the foundation for all cognitive behavior.

Human growth and development occur at different rates and it is difficult to determine when one stage begins and another ends. Indicators of human development such as the "milestones of life" that Neulinger[12] used to identify "important events, highlights, or crises that tend to be common to all or most people" are characteristics of human development. Milestones such as entering and/or finishing school, first date, first car, first job, marriage, and first child are indicators of social development and maturity. There is support for the thesis that readiness is a prerequisite for learning and that learning and instincts play a role in the development process.

In formulating the goals and objectives of a recreation program, readiness and self-confidence, combined with opportunity, are the primary determinants of human behavior. In the following age groups, there are developmental traits that provide a basis for recreation program planning. The following brief descriptions are provided as examples and the programmer should consult a developmental psychology text for the specific characteristics of each group.

Group	Age	Characteristic
Preschool	Under 4	Dependent on others, short attention span, self-centered, major motor development, and desire for immediate reward.
Primary	5 to 7	Developing social relations and additional motor skills, imagination and exuberance, develops self-control, and becomes industrious.
Intermediate	8 to 12	Perseverance, diligence, and competency develop; play is serious business.
Early adolescence	13 to 15	Rapid physical growth, onset of puberty, sometimes awkward, and self-conscious.
Youth	16 to 19	Develops individual identity, discovers talents. Strong likes and dislikes, group memberships, sets goals, and strives for independence.
Young adult	20 to 29	Seeks meaningful relationships, makes commitments, career choices, and uses a variety of recreation activities in the courtship ritual, may pursue outdoor and risk activities to test competency.
Adult years	30 to 49	Major productive years, child-rearing responsibilities and other social obligations. Looks to recreation for activity, diversion, status, and autonomy.
Pre-retirement adult	50 to 64	Reduction of intensity of some needs, generally secure, enjoys social outings, provides leadership in social-spiritual-civic and volunteer organizations.
Early retirement	65 to 79	Recreation often replaces work as reason for being. Can be active or passive, depending on health. General physical decline and more difficult to stimulate.
Later maturity	Over 80	Contingent upon health, can be a rewarding but semi passive way of life. Research has revealed that those who prepare for retirement and later maturity can prevent the despair associated with the loss of independence, isolation, and a lonely wait for death.

An understanding of the characteristics of the stages of human development provides a programmer with a basis for planning a comprehensive program. Program planning can be enhanced if the programmer understands the personalities of the individual participants. Two distinctive personality types have been identified and discussed in the literature. Type A and type B, or orientation toward achievement and affiliation, which were identified by the psychologist Cronback,[13] provide for further insight into human behavior. It is not a recreation specialist's responsibility to analyze participants' personalities; however, he or she needs a general understanding of human behavior to effectively match recreation resources with recreation needs.

MOTIVATION THEORY

For most people, recreation and leisure activities are still considered to be a reward for work, perhaps work well done. Work is a habit, reinforced by the work ethic and society's materialistic values. It leads to the satisfaction of our economic needs, and economic success is measured by earning power and/or wealth. Work is a means to an end which does not guarantee job satisfaction or happiness, especially in some depersonalized work environments. For many employees, work simply meets their economic needs and has little or no relation to their other needs. For others, work is the center of their existences and it satisfies their needs.

Social indicators point to an increasing number of people who are turning to alternative activities as a method of satisfying their physical, social, and psychological needs that were once fulfilled by work, but are no longer attainable in the workplace. Finding alternatives to work as a purpose for life presents an individual with the difficult task of breaking with tradition and habit. Alternatives to work, or nonwork endeavors, especially recreation activities that provide people with opportunities to attain personal autonomy, identity, pride, pleasurable experiences, challenges, and personal enjoyment, are replacing work as a central focus of life.

Involving people in recreation activities once they have established a lifestyle or routine is a difficult task. Involving people, and successfully promoting or marketing recreation and leisure services, requires a carefully planned strategy. Appealing to the latent urge to play, providing the rationale for, or using the right stimulus to involve people in recreation activity, requires an understanding of their needs. Often, programmers must assess recreation needs and rely on an understanding of Maslow's[14] theory of motivation to identify and relate human needs to recreation activities.

Maslow's hierarchy includes the following:

1. Physiological needs: the need for food, rest, exercise, clothing, and shelter.
2. Security needs: protection from danger, threats, and deprivation.
3. Social needs: belonging, associations, friendships, and giving and receiving love.
4. Self-esteem: ego needs, self-confidence, independence, competence, recognition, and status.
5. Self-actualization: desire for self-fulfillment to be or be more and more of what one is, to become everything that one is capable of becoming.

Maslow proposed five principles of human behavior, all of which are applicable to identifying recreation needs.

1. All human behavior has a purpose, is need-or goal-directed and, once a need is satisfied, it is no longer a driving force or motivator of behavior.
2. Human needs exist on a hierarchy in ascending order from physiological needs to higher level psychological needs. People seek first to satisfy lower level needs prior to satisfying higher level needs.
3. There are individual differences in the priority placed on needs and the manner in which people will seek to satisfy their needs.
4. People are incapable of satisfying their needs for extended periods as needs reoccur on a continuous basis.
5. Dissatisfaction causes people to change. Once a need is fulfilled or an individual is no longer challenged by the way he or she satisfies a need, that individual will turn to new activities or challenges to satisfy that or other needs.[15]

There are specific recreation activities that can be associated with the satisfaction of an individual's physical, safety, social, and other psychological needs. They are listed on page 30.

The motivation-hygiene theory proposed by Herzberg[16] has been used to identify, clarify, and explain psychological needs. Hygiene factors are environmental elements that are necessary to promote behavior. For example, recreation areas and facilities are hygiene factors, while motivators are the anticipated and attained benefits of recreation experiences.

According to Hersey and Blanchard,[17] in designing a motivating environment or situation, if you know the high strength needs (Maslow) of an individual you want to influence, you should be able to determine

Hygiene Factors	Motivators
Environments	*Activities*
Leisure service	Achievement
organizations	Recognition
Areas and facilities	Challenges
Supervision	Responsibility
Social conditions	Growth and
Interpersonal relations	development
Security	

the goals (Herzberg) you could provide in the environment to motivate those individuals. Figure 2.1 illustrates the relationship between Maslow's and Herzberg's frameworks.

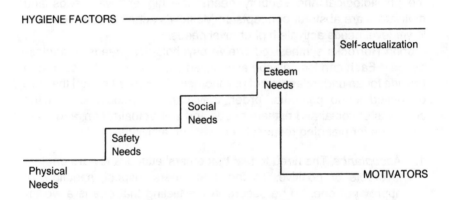

FIGURE 2.1 *Relationship between the motivation-hygiene theory and Maslow's hierarchy of needs.*

The need for physical, intellectual, and social experiences can be satisfied on each level of Maslow's hierarchy, while Herzberg's theory helps to identify the conditions that contribute to human motivation. For example, playing basketball meets the need for physical activity, yet it requires a knowledge of the rules and strategies of the game, and people play the game in an environment that promotes social inter-action. Team membership provides for meeting some security needs, some esteem, and it can provide for self-actualization. The hygiene factors in the basketball example are: a leisure-service organization, an appropriate facility, an organizer or supervisor, and game officials who control the game and reduce risk. The motivators include the opportunity to achieve success, playing the game, possibly winning, and the challenge.

Carefully planned recreation programs afford people an opportunity to satisfy a variety of their needs and provide them with inherent incentives to be involved. Program goals and objectives are formulated and programs planned by the cognitive process of internalizing anticipated recreation needs and then providing appropriate opportunities.

PSYCHOLOGICAL NEEDS

A scientific perspective of life logically classifies basic functions as physiological, social, and psychological. Herzberg's and Maslow's theories provide a means of understanding human behavior and, therefore, provide a basis for planning recreation activities. Excluding the physiological and security needs, the higher level needs and motivators are abstract concepts. In Maslow's scheme, satisfaction of lower level needs activate higher level needs.

John Horrocks synthesized twelve psychological needs of adolescence.[18] Each can logically be associated with the entire life span and provide for an understanding of psychological needs. Although they are presented in no particular order, they can be associated with the concepts of social and esteem needs and self-actualization, and used as criteria for planning responsive recreation activities.

1. *Acceptance.* The need to feel that others' attitudes toward one are favorable or positive. To feel that others respect, sanction, or approve of one. To be secure in the feeling that one is a worthy person in another's eyes. To feel that one is not rejected.
2. *Achievement.* The need to acquire, gain, receive, win, or strive to accomplish goals, tokens of status and respect, or knowledge. To attain, secure, prove, surmount through praiseworthy exertion.
3. *Affection.* The need to be loved, cherished, emotionally wanted for one's own sake; to receive unconditional love and affection. To receive emotional love from parents, relatives, friends, or lovers.
4. *Approval.* The need to have others' behavior toward one indicate that one is a satisfactory person or that one's deeds are satisfactory. To seek overt rewards or other signs of approval. To be given overt demonstrations by others of one's worthiness. To avoid blame, criticism, punishment.
5. *Belonging.* The need to feel a part of a group or institution. To identify oneself with a person, group, institution, or idea. To be a member of a congenial group.

6. *Conformity.* The need to be like others, to avoid marked departure from the mode. To yield or conform to custom. To avoid being different in dress, behavior, attitude, ideals.
7. *Dependence.* The need to have, ask for, or depend on others for emotional support, protection, care, encouragement, forgiveness, help.
8. *Independence.* The need to be free of external control by friends, family, associates, and others. To do things in a self-determining manner, to make one's decisions, to be self-sufficient, to rely on oneself.
9. *Master-dominance.* The need to control, to be in power, to lead, to manage, govern, overcome people, problems, obstacles. To influence the behavior, feelings, or ideas of others.
10. *Recognition.* The need to be noticed, to become known. To avoid effacement of one's individuality. To be identified by others as a unique individual, to be distinguished from others. To find one's place, to be regarded as an important human being.
11. *Self-realization.* The need to function at one's ability level. To learn, understand, perform to the best of one's ability; to avoid performing at a mediocre level. To strive for increasingly better accomplishment within the levels of one's capacity.
12. *To be understood.* The need to feel in sympathetic rapport with parents, relatives, friends, associates. To feel at one with others. To feel free to express one's innermost thoughts and problems to one or more persons without loss of affection or personal status. To feel that another identifies with oneself.

RECREATION BEHAVIORS

The current and predictable trend in recreation programming is to provide opportunities for the individual, with individual participants then being organized into groups. The planning of responsive activities for people individually and collectively requires an assessment of the individual's, a group's, and a community's needs. A need is a psycho-socio-physiological drive that compels an individual to act to satisfy a specific need. Recreation behavior originates from an internal drive to satisfy a need(s), and it usually consists of some form of activity, for which some generalizations can be concluded about the activity.

Murphy, Williams, Niepoth, and Brown have identified the following recreation behaviors which provide a broad base for establishing program goals and objectives, and for developing programs.[19] These behaviors should be encouraged in a manner that promotes progressive involvement in recreation and leisure activities.

1. *Socializing behavior:* relating to other people, social interactions in social environments.
2. *Acquisitive behavior:* involves the gathering or collection of items and often provides the foundations for associative behavior, the collection of antiques, baseball cards, and other items.
3. *Associative behavior:* gathering of people around a common interest, often involving a formal organization of interests, or activities.
4. *Competitive behavior:* the whole range of sports and games, usually occurring within the context of a set of rules and procedures.
5. *Testing behaviors:* the assessment of one's skills and abilities against a standard or element of nature, mountain climbing, rafting, skiing, etc.
6. *Risk-taking behaviors:* involving such activities as hang-gliding, parachuting, rappeling, or gambling.
7. Explorative behavior: seeking new experiences involving travel, hiking, scuba diving, and the study of a variety of academic subjects.
8. *Vicarious behavior:* examples are watching television, listening to music, and spectator sports.
9. Sensory stimulation: Murphy, et al. state, "all recreation behavior involves sensory stimulation to some degree. Some experiences are more dependent upon this factor than others."[20] Music, visual stimuli, eating, drinking, drugs, and sexual activities are examples of sensory activities.
10. *Physical expression:* running, jumping, striking, and climbing are physical activities involving vigorous movements. Swimming, skiing, and creative dance are others.
11. *Creative behavior:* including all of the art forms, crafts, literature, dance, and any other act that gives new meaning, expression, or use to the known and unknown.
12. *Appreciative behavior:* the participant usually responds to the product or result of the creative process rather than interacting directly. The natural environment, esthetic experiences are examples.
13. *Variety-seeking behavior:* diversion, change from the normal routine.
14. *Anticipation and recollective behavior:* preparation for planned activities and post experience recall are a part of most recreation experiences.

The behaviors listed are not mutually exclusive and any activity or recreation experience may include one or more of these behaviors.

SOCIAL BEHAVIOR

The social aspects of human behavior should be considered in the formation of a system's goals, objectives, and programs. Human behavior is influenced as much by social interactions as it is by psychological and physiological needs, because most people satisfy their needs in the social environment.

In planning recreation and leisure-service programs, an individual should be aware of the dynamic nature of our multicultured (melting pot) society and the extent to which individual behavior is influenced by cultural pluralism. Multicultured societies accept cultural pluralism as a way of life; it serves to preserve and extend cultural diversity. Cultural pluralism affirms that the unique attributes of all population groups and their opinions, attitudes, values, customs, and traditions are forces that enrich the vitality of the nation. Recreation and leisure-service systems, as a matter of policy, should promote opportunities that encourage social interactions between people of all racial and ethnic groups to foster better understanding and greater appreciation of each person's contribution to the nation's vitality. Programs of this nature ensure equal access for all people to recreation opportunities and eliminate the psychological barriers that often serve to exclude individuals from programs without due cause. Promoting opportunities in which an individual is exposed to and socially interacts in a multicultured setting provides for human development through recreation experience, a goal of the holistic perspective influencing the recreation and leisure-service movement of the 1980s and 1990s.

SUMMARY

The primary purpose of any recreation and leisure-service system is to provide opportunities for people to engage in recreation and leisure behavior. The process of providing these opportunities involves a systematic planning process that uses goals and objectives as the criteria for producing opportunities and for determining the effectiveness of the opportunities produced.

Goals are philosophical statements of general purpose or intent based upon needs, and they provide a system with general direction. Collective and organized efforts to provide socially significant opportunities for people are now influenced by a holistic understanding of recreation. This new perspective has provided a new direction for programming efforts. Contemporary programs are formulated to provide people with opportunities that contribute to their growth and development, while improving the general quality of life.

Programming efforts directed toward the attainment of recreation's holistic goals mandate that a system adopt corresponding objectives. Objectives are statements of intended action, the results of which are measurable within a time frame. Objectives, like goals, are based upon the needs of people and specify how a system can best serve the needs and interests of its constituents. Goals and objectives should always be locally oriented and based upon identifiable needs.

Seven principles for planning and conducting recreation and leisure opportunities were synthesized from the literature. The principles are as follows:

1. Recreation leadership should be provided to plan, develop, and conduct activities and programs.
2. Recreation programs should be planned to provide opportunities for the individual.
3. Recreation programs should contribute to and enhance personal development.
4. Recreation opportunities should be planned to make maximum use of available human and physical resources.
5. Natural areas; the outdoors should be planned and conserved for a variety of recreation purposes.
6. A recreation program should be subject to continuous evaluation.
7. Alternative plans for each planned activity or event in a program should be developed.

Principles are guidelines for action directed at the attainment of a goal or an objective. They are likewise based upon an understanding of human needs and the holistic perspective of recreation and leisure services. Human needs for involvement provide the foundations for organizing and providing recreation and leisure services. It is paramount to remember that needs are subject to change in relation to intensity and priority and a person's position on the life line or specific physiological, psychological, or social drives. General theories of human development, motivation, psychological needs, recreation, and social behavior were reviewed. The program planner is reminded that this is a multicultured democratic society and that all people, regardless of age, sex, racial or ethnic origin, or any other circumstance, have a right to engage in recreation and leisure behavior.

ENDNOTES

1. Gray, D.E., in J.F. Murphy (1975), Recreation and Leisure Services (p. 214). Dubuque, IA: W.C. Brown Company.
2. Gold, S.M., (December, 1979). Muddling toward frugality, Ten Type, District Ten, California Park and Recreation Society.
3. Goals and objectives. San Jose, CA: Park and Recreation Department.
4. Butler, G.D. (1967). Introduction to community recreation (pp. 260-264). New York: McGraw-Hill.
5. Danford, H.D. & Shirley, J.M. (1970). Creative leadership in recreation (pp. 125-136). Boston: Allyn and Bacon.
6. Hutchinson, J.L. (1949). Principles of recreation (pp. 178-200). New York: A.S. Barnes Company.
7. Kraus, R.G. (1977). Recreation today: Program planning and leadership (pp. 99-101). Santa Monica, CA: Goodyear Publishing Company.
8. Tillman, A. (1973). The program book for recreation professionals (p. 65). Palo Alto, CA: National Press Books.
9. Hersey, P. and Blanchard, K.H. (1977). Management of organizational behavior: utilizing human resources. (3rd ed.). Englewood Clifts, NJ: Prentice Hall, Inc.
10. Gray, D.E. (1981 March 8). Recreation experiences; paper presented at the annual meeting of the California Park and Recreation Society, San Diego.
11. Erikson, E. (1978) in Hall & Lindzey (eds.). Theories of personalities, 3rd ed. (pp. 91-100). New York: John Wiley and Sons.
12. Neulinger, J. (1981). To leisure: an introduction (pp. 157-173). Boston: Allyn and Bacon.
13. Cronback, J. (1968). Education psychology, 2nd ed., (pp. 46-52). New York: Harcourt, Brace and World, Inc.
14. Maslow, A. (1976) in R.J. Lowry (ed), A.H. Maslow an intellectual portrait (p. 28). Monterey, CA: Brooks-Cole Publishing.
15. Ibid.
16. Herzberg, F. (1966). Work and the nature of man. New York: World Publishing Company.
17. Hersey and Blanchard, p. 66.
18. Horrocks, J.E. (1962). The psychology of adolescence (2nd ed., p. 507). Boston: Houghton Miffin Company.
19. Murphy, J.F., Williams, J.G., Niepoth, E.W., and Brown, P.D. (1973). Leisure service delivery system (p. 73). Philadelphia: Lea and Febiger.
20. Ibid. p. 74.

3

APPROACHES TO PROGRAM PLANNING

Recreation programming is the process of identifying human needs, interests, and abilities and then organizing the resources necessary to produce activity opportunities and experiences that satisfy recreation needs. Providing opportunities for people to engage in recreation and leisure activities is the basic purpose of park, recreation, and leisure-service organizations and the major responsibility of recreation programmers. Considering the psychological, social, and physical aspects of the recreation experience, the programmer accepts the responsibility of providing people with a broad spectrum of opportunities. This spectrum of opportunities is so broad and diverse that it compares with individual differences, and, therefore, programmers are challenged to provide a comprehensive program that is related to and responsive to the various needs and interests of people.

Comprehensive programs consist of a vast spectrum of recreation opportunities designed to appeal to and be responsive to the individual needs, interests, and abilities of people. Recreation programs have traditionally consisted of physical, social, creative, and outdoor opportunities designed for group participation, normally by children, youth, and senior citizens. The contemporary perspective of recreation and the psychological and holistic interpretations advocated by Gray[1] and Murphy[2] have served to expand upon the traditional target groups served. Programs are now planned for everyone from infants and toddlers through senior citizens, and the disabled and other special populations are included in contemporary offerings. Today's programs are designed to enhance human growth and development and to enrich the quality of life. A vast range of activity opportunities and other services are now included in a recreation and leisure-service program.

Comprehensive programs represent extensive planning and preparation by programmers to afford all of an organization's constituents an opportunity to engage in recreation activities. Planning is the key to successful programming and the objectives of planning are to ensure that the opportunities provided are related to and responsive to people's recreation needs, interests, abilities, and desires. The programmer serves both the organization that employs him or her and the people served by the organization.

Planning and developing a recreation program is not easy; it is a process requiring an informed awareness of all the factors and variables that influence human behavior. If human behavior could be accurately predicted, recreation programming would be much easier. Human behavior is not predictable. It is subject to change in relation to the requirements of human growth and development and other situational demands that are characteristic of living in our technically advanced society, which is in a constant state of change. Therefore, the requirements for satisfying the recreation needs of people, individually and collectively, also change constantly.

The programmer's main function is to maintain an informed awareness of and sensitivity to the recreation needs of people and the factors that contribute to and influence recreation needs, interests, and abilities. The individual's needs, interests, and abilities are the basis for planning recreation programs. Conceptually, all humans require some form of recreation experience integrated into their lives. Recreation experiences may be intellectual, physical, psychological, social, and/or spiritual in origin or nature and should result in the positive experiences Gray described in his definition of recreation.[1]

Recreation involvement is related to a person's philosophy of life, culture, intellectual, physical, social, and spiritual conditioning or lifestyle, which are major determinants of the intensity of that person's recreation needs and involvement. An individual may engage in recreation daily or occasionally, and his or her involvement may range from casually listening to music to activities requiring intense concentration, advanced skills, physical conditioning, knowledge, and sophisticated equipment. A person may also pursue recreation in a variety of environments or settings and with or without the assistance of professional personnel.

Programmers planning a comprehensive program will discover that they need a thorough knowledge of recreation activities and how they are conducted. This includes a knowledge of human behavior, the personnel, equipment, supplies, facilities, and the time required to conduct all planned activities. While developing a comprehensive program, one or more programmers may be involved in planning, and plans must be consistent with an agency's goals and the recreation needs of constituents. Whether one or more programmers plan a program, comprehensive programs are expected and the programmers involved may be specialists in one or more program areas: arts and crafts; aquatics; dance; drama; music; outdoor recreation, including camping and nature study; and sports, athletics, and games. The planning effort may be directed at target groups and place special emphasis on the needs of children; youth; young adults; senior citizens; special populations; or employee activities, entertainment, adventure and risk recreation, and social recreation activities. When an agency is responsible for a comprehensive program, the programmer must plan and implement all of the activities within a reasonable time period and on an annual, seasonal, or quarterly basis, as required by the people served. In all program-planning situations, the programmer is responsible for developing opportunities that allow for the progressive development of skills, interests, and abilities in an enjoyable atmosphere.

It should be understood that a recreation and leisure-service agency's goals and objectives are generally compatible with the needs of the people served. Therefore, the principles of recreation outlined in chapter 2 are guidelines for planning, organizing, and conducting activities that contribute to the satisfaction of people's needs. Sixteen program-planning strategies have been identified in the recent literature. Ideally, each could be considered as the interactive process of the systems approach to recreation programming. The program-planning and delivery strategies outlined in this section can be used to guide the system's interactive processes, and are alternatives to the systems approach to program planning. Aspects of each method or strategy for program planning have been incorporated into the systems approach explained in detail in chapters 4 through 11. Each of the planning methods that will be reviewed was designed to achieve the goals and objectives of a park and recreation department.

Although successful, the program-planning methods and delivery strategies identified in the recent literature are enhanced by the systems approach, which is designed to be more responsive to participant and potential participant needs and change than some of the other planning methods. In addition to the systems approach, the sixteen methods have been placed into two categories: planning methods and procedures, and delivery strategies. An overview of the systems approach is presented following a review of the other approaches to recreation program planning.

PLANNING METHODS AND PROCEDURES

Program-planning methods and procedures are basically administrative processes for organizing, developing, and implementing recreation activities. Farrell and Lundegren[3] state that program planning is a process and have developed a program classification system, which provides a method of giving full attention to the development of a comprehensive program. According to Farrell and Lundegren, the popular method of classifying recreation activities is to define them by discipline or profession, "that is, art, crafts, dance, drama, hobbies, literary activities, music, environmental activities, social recreation, and sports and athletics," which they identified as the functional program classification system. The other classifications they suggest are:

1. Facilities required.
2. Number of people required to do the activity or social interaction.
3. Age group.
4. Time availability.
5. Motivation and interest.
6. Expected outcomes.

The flowchart method, synergetic programming, and community involvement strategy are the most recent planning methods advocated to enhance the planning process and the delivery of services. The creative plan identified by Tillman[4] and the prescriptive approach identified by Murphy, Williams, Niepoth, and Brown[5] contribute to the systems approach. The traditional, authoritarian, current practice, and expressed desire methods, each originally identified by Danford,[6] the investigation and reaction plans by Tillman,[4] and the educated-guess and other procedures identified by Edginton and Hanson[7] all provide the foundations from which the systems approach has evolved.

THE FLOW CHART METHOD

The flowchart method (FCM) was developed by Murphy and Howard.[8] It identified all the tasks involved in planning, organizing, and evaluating recreation programs using a flowchart. The process consists of six steps. A brief description and discussion of the method follows.

Identification of Needs and Interests

Murphy and Howard suggest a systematic approach to a comprehensive recreation survey to collect data on:

1. Expressed needs and interests.
2. Attitudes and opinions.
3. Resources available.
4. Demographical data.

A formula for comparing needs with resources is suggested. The "need index" developed by Staley provides a solid and objective planning tool for the intellectual allocation of program resources. The variables used in calculating the "need index" are population, population density, median family income, and delinquency or crime rate per neighborhood or community.

The resource index consists of the number of full and part-time professional staff per 1,000 population per year in a neighborhood; acreage of neighborhood recreation centers per one thousand (1,000) population and/or population/acreage standard; and the number of recreation centers with staff per 10,000 population.

The formula used to determine comparative priority needs for a neighborhood recreation center is recreation resources minus the need index which equals comparative priority for service.

Staff Coordination and Preparation

The second phase is staff planning and organizing activities. The needs information is translated into specific option plans in the form of programs and services. New programs and the modification of existing offerings are staff tasks involved in the second stage. Manpower, fiscal resources, materials, time, facilities, and publicity requirements are details coordinated by the FCM.

Policy-Making Body Approval

The approval, which occurs after staff agreement and prior to implementation, is the most critical, especially if additional money or new directions in service orientation are needed or intended. Written policy statements reflecting the goals and objectives of the agency are necessary to guide the policy-making board or commission, or owners in commercial recreation.

Citizen Involvement

The central element in the program-planning process is the advisory council, which acts as the go-between for the community's residents and the professional staff.

Conduct the Program

The implementation of the program phase.

Evaluation

Assessment of the effectiveness of the program. A systematic process of analyzing feedback from staff personnel and participants to determine the effectiveness of the planned activities.

Murphy and Howard[8] introduced the FCM as an organizational tool to be used by recreation staff in organizing and implementing a particular recreation activity or event. It is a technique that attempts to eliminate oversight and uncertainty in the planning process. Basically, it is a systematic forecasting process that attempts to account for and sequentially set a precedent for each work requirement in the organization of a recreation program. The FCM begins by dividing the entire program into its essential components. In the process, the planner identifies the major requirements for completion of the program. Five major functions identified by the FCM are manpower, material, facilities, program, and publicity. A random list of tasks is developed for each function and priorities are set for the various activities within each of the major planning functions.

The next step in the process is to project a time line, which represents the estimated length of time necessary to complete all the planning requirements. The FCM places the planner in a position to anticipate and prevent potential problems, and it enables delegation of responsibilities to subordinates.

The authors of the FCM have suggested that it is eminently superior to many other planning and nonplanning approaches, although it is time-consuming and subject to human error. The FCM is more complicated than other program-planning methods advocated in current literature and it closely resembles the systems approach to recreation program planning.

SYNERGETIC PROGRAMMING

Synergetic programming, according to Dunn and Phillips, is "the process of combining the unique resources of more than one agency to produce leisure services which could not be carried out successfully by one agency alone."[9] The procedures were suggested by the late George Hjelte[10] in the early 1940s; again in 1963 by Carlson, Deppe, and MacLean;[11] and several other individuals and agencies in the 1970s. Synergetic programming has become increasingly popular as resources decline and there are limited resources to support recreation programs.

There are two basic approaches to synergetic programming: the interagency approach and the cooperative funding approach. The first consists of intergovernment cooperation. The unique resources of the park and recreation department are combined with those of other public agencies—health, education, housing, human services, police, and manpower agencies—and the facilities and equipment of all governmental agencies are used to produce recreation and other human services that otherwise could not be provided by a single agency acting alone. The second approach is cooperation between public, private, commercial, and voluntary agencies for funding, use of physical facilities and resources, and the promotion of activities.

Examples of intergovernment and interagency cooperation are numerous, including the cooperative venture into metropolitan housing and recreation complexes, school-community centers, and community schools in the public sector. The 1984 Olympics in Los Angeles was a prime example of interagency cooperation involving the Los Angeles Olympic Organizing Committee; The City of Los Angeles; The University of California at Los Angeles; University of Southern California; and other state and local jurisdictions, private agencies, and corporate sponsors of the Olympic Games.

The use of volunteers; the temporary assignment of personnel to other divisions and agencies; and the sponsorship of recreation leagues, tournaments, track and field meets, and other activities such as art festivals and concerts are basic forms of synergetic programming. Without the additional resources realized through synergetic effort, recreation programs in many communities would be seriously limited.

According to Dunn and Phillips,[9] synergetic programming has three important attributes:

1. Stretching the public dollar.
2. Enhancing public relations.
3. Helping to keep the department dynamic.

Synergetic programming enables an agency to explore all possible alternatives when considering ways and means of developing, supervising, and supporting recreation services. When a program idea is suggested, cooperative efforts enable the agency to employ four alternative strategies[4]:

1. An extra-agency program.
2. Synergetic programming.
3. Recreation agency program.
4. No program.

Synergetic programming is an administrative process for generating fiscal support and for enlisting interagency cooperation. When these methods are used, program evaluation is the final phase and a program can be continued or discontinued, depending upon continued support and the needs and interests of the agency's constituents. Dunn and Phillips researched urban recreation situations and focused their attention on urban financial problems.

They state,

> Today, isolation by urban recreation agencies is not only unjustifiable philosophically; it is untenable at the practical level. In addition to the diminishing municipal budget, growing operational and maintenance cost, and rising inflation, federal revenue sharing is compelling all local services to demonstrate their respective contributions to the quality of life.[9]

Synergetic programming is a common-sense method of increasing efficiency and effectiveness of all recreation agencies. Every individual employed by a park and recreation department is a potential agent for initiating a synergetic programming effort.

COMMUNITY INVOLVEMENT APPROACHES

Citizen input into the planning and allocation of funds for recreation services is a trademark of a democratic society. Beginning in the 1950s, the rapid expansion and growth of all levels of government has resulted in the creation of bureaucracies. Bureaucracies tend to remove people from the decision-making processes that affect their lives and cause them to lose confidence in government. In the 1960s, the federal government, through the War on Poverty, initiated guidelines requiring maximum feasible citizen participation in the decision-making process to ensure that federal funds would be used to alleviate social and economic problems in targeted areas. Maximum feasible citizen participation was a local requirement for many federal grant programs.

The funding criteria established by the federal government prompted municipal park and recreation departments to use their citizen boards, commissions, and advisory councils more effectively in the planning process. Park and recreation departments have also decentralized their administrations to enable local constituents to participate in the decision-making process when the decision affects the delivery of neighborhood services. Gold has been a proponent of "advocate planning" as a method of involving citizens that the program, services, and facilities are intended to serve.[12]

Providing people with an opportunity to participate in the planning and decision-making process creates a sense of community identity and pride. Community involvement allows for a valid assessment of recreation needs because a wider and more representative group of citizens is encouraged to participate as members of advisory councils and program planning committees.

Community Leadership Input

This method is one of the most widely used procedures for planning recreation programs in the profession. Edginton and Hanson defined and summarized the community leadership input method as follows:

> It has been suggested that the source of any leisure and recreation program is dependent upon involvement with the consumers it serves. One method of determining consumer needs and interests is to set up advisory and policy-making boards which represent the concerns of the public at large. Based upon the need to improve communications between the providers of service and the consumers, this approach assumes that each individual's interests will be represented by a select group of people.

> The problems inherent in this approach are numerous and, in one way or another, have involved most professionals. It is unwise to assume that a group of selected individuals, especially those thrust into positions of community leadership, will be able to represent the needs of all persons within a given service area. However, this form of community interaction with the providers of service is based on sound democratic principles and undoubtedly has merit. It is also the most common approach to opening channels of communication between the providers and consumers of services.[7]

The community leadership input theory is in actual use by program planners and is closely followed by the socio-political and the expressed-desire methods of program planning.

A fourth method of planning characteristic of this group is the reaction plan. This method is currently used in many communities and involves the programmers, who react to the demands and suggestions of their constituents and then develop recreation opportunities, without evaluating the effects of their efforts or decisions.

Socio-Political Method

Kraus and Curtis identified this approach to program planning.[13] The procedures are very similar to those of the reaction plan. Essentially, the socio-political method involves organized groups in a community that attempt to influence the allocation of resources, the development of facilities, and the delivery of services by putting social and political pressure on programmers. In most communities, park and recreation directors are confronted by groups that conduct campaigns designed to influence the allocation of resources and the delivery of services. Parks and recreation agencies exist to serve people and must respond to their recreation needs by providing programs, services, and facilities; however, no group in a community should gain an advantage over another group by using pressure tactics in their attempt to secure recreation services.

Political interest and social pressure groups do not constitute program-planning methods; nevertheless, they represent community input that influences the planning of recreation opportunities in many communities. A planner must be aware of attempts to influence the decision-making process involved in program planning and the political realities that affect program delivery.

Consumer Input Methods

The "expressed-desire method," the "reaction plan," and the "investigation plan" identified by Danford[6] and Tillman,[4] respectively, are planning methods improved upon by community involvement methods. They rely on input by the consumer of service through community surveys and the administration of interests inventories to gather information about the needs, interests, abilities, and experiences of people and what they would like an agency to offer. The expressed-desire and investigation methods actively seek information, while the reaction plan is a passive approach designed to obtain the same results.

Danford and Shirley[14] have cautioned programmers that, individually, the "expressed-desire," "current-practice," and "the authoritarian and traditional" methods of program planning should not be accepted as thoroughly sound, but they can be a part of a composite planning procedure. They have provided two important principles to consider in the program-planning process.

1. The recreation interests and desires of people are limited to their past experiences.
2. One of the most important functions of leadership is to lead people from where they are into new interests and activities which enrich life beyond anything they have ever known before.

Contemporary and future programmers have the responsibility of planning programs that contribute to the improvement of the quality of life; however, when the constituent is beyond the teen years, the incentives to participate are inner-directed rather than outer-directed by parents, teachers, recreation leaders, and others in a community.

Considering that working adults have specific needs, interests, skills, and often limited time for recreation, programmers have a responsibility to open avenues of communication with adults to enhance their opportunities for recreation enjoyment. Open communications with all constituents provide an opportunity for direct input into the program-planning process; this enhances an agency's program offerings for all the populations served. This is the intent of community involvement program-planning procedures.

PLANNING PROCEDURES

The Creative Plan

Tillman developed the creative plan by combining elements of the reaction and the investigation plans. He proposed that

> The creative plan begins with the complete, unabridged, encyclopedic collection of every possible human experience that may be improved by programming and which falls within the leisure category; i.e., which is nonsurvival-oriented, freely chosen, personally constructive, socially acceptable, and pleasurable.[4]

The plan consists of assimilating demands for programs with the result of research and the programmer's knowledge of activities and experience. Data from these sources are synthesized into a plan that conceptually meets and exceeds the constituent's needs and expectations. This plan differs just slightly in procedure from the systems approach and the flowchart method.

The Prescriptive Approach

This approach to program development was identified by Murphy et al. and is similar to many therapeutic recreation programming procedures. The agency "defines rather specific objectives to be achieved" and activities are selected that will promote the desired behaviors or values. Aspects of this procedure are found in every approach to recreation programming and especially in rehabilitation programs. The authors suggest that "specific outcomes of recreation programming and those which serve to illustrate this approach are: the enhancement of educative process, socialization of participants, facilitation of diagnostic and cathartic processes, counteracting destructive behavior, etc."[5] This approach often involves an assessment of an individual's or a group's behavior and analysis of the activity components of the program. Refer to a therapeutic recreation text for specific information on activity analysis.

OTHER PROGRAM-PLANNING METHODS

The Traditional Approach

According to Danford, programs are planned on the basis of what has been done in the past, and activities are repeated year in and year out.[6] Butler suggested that traditional activities are a logical starting point, since activities that have been successfully provided in the past provide a sound planning base.[15]

The Current Practice Approach

This is the third of the methods identified by Danford; it is essentially the process of copying what is being done in other communities and agencies, rather than attempting to initiate activities through independent planning. This method has been critized as being ineffective; however, the sharing of ideas and adapting them to local needs has enabled many communities to expand the scope of their program offerings.

The Educated-Guess Approach

This theory, identified by Edginton and Hanson,[7] is widely practiced by an increasing number of trained professionals. Activities are planned, organized, and implemented on someone's hunch that they will meet community needs. The value of this approach is that, when planning or revising a program, an educated guess can serve as the starting point for the development or revision of a program, and can lead to a successful program when an idea is subjected to careful analysis and evaluation in subsequent planning stages.

DELIVERY STRATEGIES

PRIMARY STRATEGIES

The program-planning process is not completed until recreation opportunities are provided for people's involvement and subsequently evaluated. The strategies for transforming plans into recreation experiences are as important as the actual planning process. The procedures for delivering and distributing recreation services are discussed by Murphy et al. in detail.[5] Recreation activities are delivered on a continuum, ranging from direct services to outreach or enabling services. The idea of direct and enabling services was explained by Murphy et al.

The direct service approach determines or makes some assumptions about people's recreation desires and interests; the resources are then provided, ready to be used. The enabling approach serves as a catalyst, and helps people to implement their desires and interests. It assists people in planning and obtaining needed resources; in some cases, it provides resources, which might include organizational skills, training, equipment, and areas and facilities.[5]

The provision of direct services usually involves active participation by professional personnel in the delivery of recreation opportunities. The activities are planned and directed by personnel. An example of a direct service is a playground leader conducting group games; another is a swimming instructor teaching. Enabling services on the other end of the continuum represent activities that occur without professional leadership being involved. Examples of enabling services are opportunities for family picnics, jogging in a recreation area, and groups of people using available areas and facilities on their own (i.e., children playing on apparatus, pickup basketball games, and other nondirected recreation activities).

Outreach programs are conceptually in the middle of the continuum and extend recreation services to people in their immediate environments. They involve aspects of both directed and enabling services and provide an agency with a method of extending services beyond its immediate boundaries and to people who otherwise would not receive services.

Delivery strategies are planned to (1) provide opportunities that improve direct and immediate participation and (2) provide services that enable people to develop their own opportunities. Farrell and Lundegren have proposed a program structure format for participation in recreation that consists of five delivery strategies:

1. Clinics, workshops, and classes.
2. Tournaments, contests, and leagues.
3. Clubs or interest groups.
4. Special events or performances.
5. Open facilities.[3]

Most recreation activities can be planned to use one of the five delivery strategies; however, there are three additional strategies to consider: the cafeteria approach identified by Murphy et al. and the most recent additions identified by Edginton and Hanson—indigenous development and interative discovery.

THE CAFETERIA APPROACH

This is a delivery strategy in which the agency plans and develops a wide range of activities for the public that it serves. The consumers are then expected to pick and choose "cafeteria style" from a variety of available activities, which are planned with respect to their broad appeal. People are also expected to engage in activities of their own choosing. Activities are planned to appeal to the interests, skills, and ability levels of participants. Normally, most of the activities are supervised by staff personnel and the areas and facilities are kept free of hazards to ensure adequate opportunities and personal safety.

There are elements of both directed and enabling services found in the cafeteria approach. Direct services involve activities that are planned and conducted by agency personnel for participants. Enabling services exist when the broadest range of possible activities, services, and facilities are planned and individuals are provided opportunities to use them at their own discretion. A potential shortcoming of the cafeteria approach is the inclusion of and promotion of every possible activity at each and every recreation facility. It is conceivable that a programmer using this approach would provide a variety of activities at each facility on the assumption that participants would be interested in one or more of the offerings. Considering the projected scarcity of economic resources in the 1980s, it is not feasible to use the cafeteria approach at every facility. The alternative is to provide, within the community, the broadest possible range of activities at designated facilities. Thus, the intent of the cafeteria approach is retained within the community as a whole.

The cafeteria-style program provides the consumer with a variety of alternatives for recreation involvement, in fact with many opportunities that would not be available if the idea was not considered in the planning process.

INDIGENOUS DEVELOPMENT AND INTERACTIVE DISCOVERY

Edginton and Hanson identified indigenous development and interactive discovery theories in their research; they are relatively new approaches and are people "to" people or enabling services to program development and delivery. Edginton and Hanson state:

Indigenous, within this context, is defined as the inherent needs of consumers. Indigenous development is, therefore, a process directed towards helping individuals discover and use grass root program opportunities which utilize innate capabilities and are directed towards individual needs. It is the process of planning with one's environment and life style as the focal point. This plan involves meeting people on their own terms, and it ensures that the consumers of service are involved in the planning process and have control over program offerings.[7]

This approach to program development requires the agency to utilize its professional staff and grant them freedom to develop programs that are directly related to the needs and interests of its constituents. Constituents and recreation staff personnel assume responsibility for developing activities that are needed in a neighborhood or community. Within this concept there are characteristics of enabling services, direct services, community involvement, and other program-planning methods.

The indigenous development theory places the recreation leader in the position of being an enabler, rather than an activity leader, director, or supervisor. Constant interaction is required among agency staff members to provide the agency with some understanding about what is going on and to provide some control over the activities it sponsors or sanctions. According to Edginton and Hanson, this approach to program development rewards participants psychologically, because they are directly involved in the planning, organizing, and conduct of recreation activities in their communities.

The interactive discovery theory, also identified by Edginton and Hanson, is an "extension, elaboration, and continuation of the indigenous development concept." Further, Edginton and Hanson added the following:

> Interactive discovery is based on the assumption that people can work together, interacting to discover and recognize one another as individuals. By developing a relationship of trust, based on an open and effective communication, individuals can create avenues for exchange. One individual's knowledge, skill and abilities can be used to meet another's needs, without necessarily superimposing a value system or set of expectations on either person.[7]

Interactive discovery is the purest of the enabling services approaches to program delivery. This approach and the indigenous development concept are strategies that involve the participant in the planning and implementation of activities in cooperation with recreation professionals. Participants are enabled to engage in meaningful activities, those selected and motivated by participants themselves, which ensures responsiveness and agency effectiveness in meeting the recreation needs of its constituency.

It is most likely that recreation personnel will be required to promote interactions among and between the various population groupings before an agency can effectively use either indigenous development or interactive discovery program planning and delivery strategies.

The program-planning method and delivery strategies reviewed provide an overview of procedures that can be used systemtically to plan, organize, and deliver recreation services.

THE SYSTEMS APPROACH TO RECREATION PROGRAMMING

The public, private, commercial, and voluntary agencies that provide recreation and leisure services are basically open social service systems. They serve, interpret, and act on information related to recreation needs, interests, desires, expectations, and resources in an interactive transformation process that produces recreation opportunities. The history of the park and recreation movement reveals that it began as a reaction to social conditions, has subsequently served as a preventative force, and is now an action-oriented movement that seeks to contribute to human development and to enrich the quality of life. Recreation and leisure-service systems are maintained to respond to the needs, interests, and social demands of people, and to represent society's awareness and willingness to provide resources for the following:

1. To conserve and preserve for future generations places of natural beauty and historical significance.
2. To consider social conditions, human values, and people's needs, interests, and demand for leisure.
3. To provide open space in urban settings for parks and recreation facilities to enhance opportunities for leisure experiences and play and recreation activities, including creative experiences, cultural expression, physical activity, and social interactions.
4. To provide recreation opportunities for the handicapped, aged, and other special members of society.
5. To provide recreation and leisure services as an alternative to antisocial behavior, enhancing opportunities for human expression and using diversionary activities to control, prevent, and discourage delinquent and criminal behavior.
6. To provide for leisure and recreation education.
7. To provide an opportunity to earn a profit by agencies offering pleasurable, entertaining, challenging, risk, or exciting experiences. Economic incentives are normally associated with the private and commercial sectors of recreation services.

The systems approach to recreation programming is an open social system that plans, organizes, develops, implements, controls, and evaluates recreation activities and programs in relation to people's needs, interests, abilities, expectations, and available resources. It is a process that attempts to maintain effective human relationships while providing for scientific accuracy in transforming needs, resources, and technical data into recreation and leisure opportunities. The process leads to the production of a variety of opportunities for recreation and leisure experiences.

The recreation program represents all of the activity opportunities, services, and facilities provided by an agency.

In all planning situations, whether one activity or a total array of activities and events are planned, a number of interactions and relationships are systematically involved and regulated by the planning process.

The systems approach integrates operational, managerial, and instructional systems theory and practice into a composite planning process. It is a synthesis of related theories and planning methods into a process that is effective and efficient in the use of resources in providing recreation services. The process uses a system's goals and objectives as the basis of its planning procedure.

The basic design of a system is illustrated by Figure 3.1, the systems approach to recreation program planning. The design illustrates that the system receives input from its environment—basic data pertaining to recreation needs and resources (human, fiscal, and physical)—which is processed in the interactions-transformation phase to produce output. The process consists of an analysis of recreation needs and resources in relation to the system's goals and objectives and by its subsystem components. The process or interactive-transformation phase produces output, that is, opportunities for recreation experiences.

FIGURE 3.1 *The systems approach to recreation programming.*

The major subsystem components of a social system have been described by Hersey and Blanchard.[16] They are as follows:

1. The administrative/structural subsystem. The systems administrator is responsible for activating the system and its resources and for guiding it toward the attainment of its goals and objectives. The basic purpose of a park and recreation service system is to provide people opportunities to engage in recreation and leisure behavior. The system's goals give it a purpose and influence its administrative, physical, and operational functions and structure.
2. The information/decision-making subsystem. The system functions as an information-gathering and procession decision-making process. This subsystem is designed to seek, receive, and analyze data pertaining to the operations of recreation services and make operational decisions in relation to and in the interests of attaining its goals and objectives.
3. The economic/technical subsystem. This subsystem controls fiscal resources and prescribes the technical procedures used in planning, organizing, controlling, and evaluating the system's operations.
4. The social/human subsystem. The human component is the subsystem that gives meaning, purpose, and direction and makes the system functional. Humans bring to the system the knowledge and technical skills by performing the duties and responsibilities inherent in program planning and delivery.

The intermediate design of the program-planning process is illustrated by Figure 3.2, which is intended to depict interactions between goals and objectives, the subsystems, recreation needs, and resources. Instructional systems theory is applied in the intermediate design on the assumption that individuals can be described in terms of manifested behavior, and that visual changes in human behavior can result from recreation and leisure experiences.

Goals and objectives provide the system with guidelines for structuring and controlling the interactions between the subsystem components. Humans provide the system with the element capable of performing its administrative, technical, and decision-making functions.

The systems approach to program planning requires the programmer to identify and analyze recreation needs and resources. This enables him or her to forecast and plan in advance a variety of activity opportunities and to select the most responsive activities for immediate implementation. In the process, needs and resources are identified, analyzed, classified, and evaluated by the system's subsystem components. The interactions between needs, resources, goals, and objectives, and the subsystems produce additional data and internal feedback for evaluation and consideration prior to the implementation of services. The process is graphically illustrated by Figure 3.3.

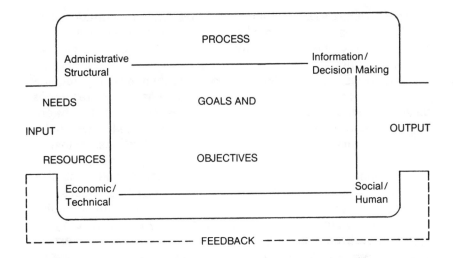

FIGURE 3.2 *Intermediate design of the systems approach to recreation program planning.*

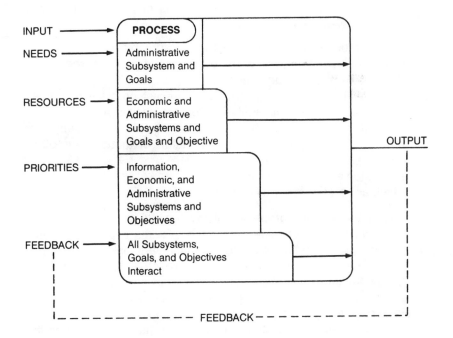

FIGURE 3.3 *Systems-subsystems interactions.*

This approach is constantly activated by input or feedback, which enable priorities for action to be established on the basis of a needs-resource index and the decision to be reached to implement an activity or program.

The systems approach to recreation program planning requires programmers to identify and analyze recreation needs and resources, cause-and-effect relationships, costs and benefits, and activity and facility capacity, every conceivable factor and variable involved in the process. Community involvement is encouraged to ensure that all factors and variables are considered in the planning process.

The planning, organizing, promoting, conducting, and controlling process is accomplished in seven sequential planning phases. The process is initiated by input or administrative directive. Administrative approval is required prior to implementating any activity or program, initiating new programs, hiring new leadership personnel, and expending funds to provide for administrative accountability. The systems approach enables planners to justify new programs, revise existing programs, and eliminate ineffective programs. It is a planning and decision-making process that helps programmers develop relevant and responsive recreation opportunities for people, and it involves interactions between the system and its environment to produce a plan that effectively uses resources to meet the needs of people. The seven phases of the systems approach are:

1. Definition of the system's purpose, goals, and objectives.
2. Identification and analysis of recreation needs and resources.
3. Development of program objectives.
4. Determination of program cost and forecast program outcomes (activity and cost-benefit analysis, program feasibility).
5. Operational planning, the detailed scheduling, allocation of resources, processing, and coordination of human and other resources.
6. Promotion and implementation.
7. Feedback and continuous evaluation.

The sequential design is graphically illustrated by Figure 3.4.

Programmers who consider using the systems approach to programming are not confronted with the immediate task of planning a completely new program. The systems approach is initially used as a procedure for improving the effectiveness and efficiency of existing programs. Organizations adopting systems procedures will not suspend all activities one day and initiate new activities the next; they will use the procedures to evaluate existing programs and use the results as the basis for continuing, revising, or eliminating activities, and implementing new activities without interrupting existing services. Subsequently, the systems approach is used as a tool for forecasting and planning all the activities to be promoted by an organization.

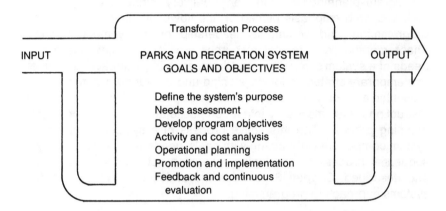

INPUT

Transformation Process

PARKS AND RECREATION SYSTEM
GOALS AND OBJECTIVES

Define the system's purpose
Needs assessment
Develop program objectives
Activity and cost analysis
Operational planning
Promotion and implementation
Feedback and continuous
    evaluation

OUTPUT

FIGURE 3.4   *Process design for developing a recreation activity or program.*

The sequential processes involved in the systems approach are influenced by an organization's goals and objectives and the environment in which it exists. Its effectiveness is determined by the performance of its subsystems, and by the effect that the social, political, economic, and physical environments have on its internal functions as resources are allocated to provide recreation opportunities that are responsive and related to people's needs, interests, abilities, recreational skills, and expectations. All planned recreation services are intended to provide experiences that contribute to human development and the quality of life.

SUMMARY

Recreation programming is the process of identifying people's needs and then organizing the resources necessary to produce recreation opportunities that satisfy those needs. Contemporary programs attempt to go beyond providing activities to providing experiences that contribute to the growth and development of the individual and concurrently serve to enrich the quality of life.

Recreation programs are the sum total of all activity opportunities planned, organized, and provided by an agency for the pleasure and enjoyment of people. They normally consist of a vast array of different activities provided for people of all ages and both sexes, and other human conditions or circumstances.

Program-planning methods and delivery strategies have been reviewed, with emphasis placed on the flowchart method, synergetic programming, and community leadership or involvement theories. These methods ensure that resources are used to meet the actual needs of a system's constituents. Direct, enabling, outreach, and other contemporary strategies for developing and delivering programs were presented as a foundation for synthesizing operational, managerial, and instructional systems theory into a composite and functional program-planning process. The interactive process of a system's major subsystem components interacting with goals, needs, and resources in the sequential process of developing recreation activities was illustrated and described. Chapter 3 provides a foundation for chapter 4, the systems approach to programming.

ENDNOTES

1. Gray, D. E., (December 12, 1971). Recreation: An Interpretation (Summary of research findings). Long Beach, CA: California State University.
2. Murphy, J. F. (1975). Recreation and leisure services (pp. 8-9). Dubuque, IA: W. C. Brown Company.
3. Farrell, P. and Lundegren, H. M. (1978). The process of recreation programming (p. 6). New York: John Wiley and Sons.
4. Tillman, A. (1973). The program book for recreation professionals (p. 58). Palo Alto, CA: National Press Books.
5. Murphy, J. F., Williams, J. G., Niepoth, E. W., and Brown, P. D. (1973). Leisure service delivery system (p. 73). Philadelphia: Lea & Febiger.
6. Danford, H. G. (1964). Creative leadership in recreation (pp. 104-198). Boston: Allyn & Bacon.
7. Edginton, C. R., and Hanson, C. J. (March 1876). Appraising leisure service delivery. *Parks & recreation,* 11. (3) p. 27.
8. Murphy, J. F. and Howard, D. R. (1977). Delivery of community leisure services: An holistic approach (pp. 199-203). Philadelphia: Lea & Febiger.
9. Dunn, D. R. and Phillips, L. A. (March 1975) Synergetic Programming. *Parks & recreation,* 10 (3).
10. Hjelte, G. (1940). The administration of public recreation (p. 119). New York: McMillian Company.
11. Carlson, R. E., Deppe, T. R., and MacLean, J. R. (1963). Recreation in american life (p. 240). Belmont, CA: Wadsworth Publishing Company.

12. Gold, S. M. (1973). Urban Recreation Planning (p. 11). Philadelphia: Lea & Febiger.
13. Kraus, R. G. and Curtis, J. E. (1973). Creative administration of recreation and parks (p. 86). St. Louis: C. V. Mosby.
14. Danford, H. D. and Shirley, J. M. (1970). Creative leadership in recreation, (2nd ed., p. 111). Boston: Allyn & Bacon.
15. Butler, G. (1967). Introduction to community recreation (4th ed., p. 279). New York: McGraw-Hill.
16. Hersey, P. and Blanchard, K. H. (1977). Management of organizational behavior, (3rd ed., p. 7). Englewood Cliffs, N. J.: Prentice Hall, Inc.

4

THE SYSTEMS APPROACH TO RECREATION PROGRAMMING

Organized recreation and leisure services represent the ability of society to recognize, and its willingness to respond to, the recreation needs of people. In the preceding chapters, several inferences were made to imply that park and recreation and leisure-service organizations are special kinds of systems. These organizations function as a composite of social, behavioral, instructional, managerial, and operational systems. The systems approach to recreation programming is a systematic process that enables a programmer to plan programs in response to people's needs. This is in contrast to other planning methods that provide activities and attempt to fit people into the activities or programs. The systems approach is basically a social system that exists in any organization in which people contribute to the attainment of its goals.

A social system promotes interactions among an organization's personnel and controls the efforts of individuals as they are influenced by an organization's environment. The systematic interactions enable an organization to perform the special tasks and functions required to produce output, recreation programs, and leisure services. Recreation and leisure-service organizations, whether public, private, or commercial, are special systems designed to acquire resources and provide people with programs, services, and facilities in response to their needs.

Systems processes are used to identify, analyze, and explain the internal functions and external relationships of organizations involved in the provision of recreation and leisure services. Systems procedures are used to examine and explain the cause-and-effect relationships between an organization and its environment and the organization's effectiveness in achieving its predetermined purposes. The continuous interaction of an organization and its component parts with its environment in the production of recreation and leisure services creates an identity for the system. The (input)-(process)-(output) action that enables a system to transform needs, resources, and goals into recreation opportunities is characteristic of a social system.

This chapter provides a brief analysis of systems theory and a critique of general systems theory to provide a foundation for relating and applying systems theory and procedures to the recreation program-planning process. The following chapters will provide an in-depth analysis of the systems processes involved in the development and implementation of recreation and leisure-service programs.

GENERAL SYSTEMS THEORY

Systems theory concerns itself with analysis of the components of any given system, the relationships of its components, and their interactions within and with the system's environments. It is understood that a system is different from the sum of its parts, and that recreation and leisure experiences are likewise different from the organizations that provide them and the program-planning process.

General systems theory provides for a holistic and integrated approach to explaining the relationships, interactions, and interdependence of the things to which man has given meaning and purpose. It explains and illustrates the relationships between people, the physical environment, social systems, and recreation and leisure-service agencies. Planned recreation and leisure programs, services, and facilities would not exist without organizations, and organizations could not exist without social and physical environments creating support for and a need for these services.

CHARACTERISTICS OF A SYSTEM

A basic characteristic of park, recreation, and leisure-service delivery systems is that they openly interact with people, individually and collectively, and the physical environment in planning and providing programs, services, and facilities. They receive input (resources and information) and process data through their subsystems to plan and provide recreation and leisure opportunities for people. Normally, each subsystem—administrative, information, decision-making, economic-technical, and social-human—is involved in the interactions that produce output. Output represents the achievement of a systems purpose. A subsystem or the component parts of a system can be defined as a work unit, group, or an individual with specific organizational responsibilities.

Characteristic of any system is the network of interrelated and interdependent activities that often overlap responsibilities within a system's boundaries. The interdependency associated with the subsystem's interacting with a system's goals and objectives enables a planning system to be highly sensitive to the needs of its parts and its environment and constituency. Open social systems are by design conscious of and respond to the needs, wants, and desires of the people they serve.

The boundaries of a recreation and leisure-service system are defined as the area from which it receives its resources and in which it provides programs, services, and facilities. The social and physical environments surrounding a system are the sources of its resources and general purpose. Resources for a social system include personnel, fiscal support, material, and areas and facilities. Information in this context relates to human needs and a system's goals and objectives, which provide it with general direction and purpose. The transformation of resources and information into recreation and leisure opportunities by the interdependent and interrelated activities of an organization is characteristic of a systems process.

Systems have unique characteristics and terms to describe them. The basic characteristics and terms are as follows:

1. *Equalfinality.* Equalfinality is the ability of a system to produce recreation programs, services, and facilities by starting a project in separate subsystem components and using different subsystems to produce desired outcomes without involving an entire system. In the operation of a park and recreation department, for example, a community center's basketball program would not involve parks personnel and, likewise, park personnel planting trees would not involve recreation personnel scheduling basketball officials.

2. *Differentiation.* This is the natural tendency of the system to grow and expand by taking on new responsibilities, according to Owen, Page, and Zimmerman.[1] Systems become more complex by

increasing in size, responsibility, and specialization. Park and recreation departments originally provided playground programs for children. The addition of swimming pools and learn-to-swim programs, summer sports leagues, art festivals, community theatres, day camps, and specialized programs for the disabled have expanded and extended programs, added responsibilities, and required specialization in their operations.

3. *Negative entropy.* A characteristic of a system identified by Owen, Page, and Zimmerman,[1] negative netropy is the capacity of a system to perpetuate itself by taking in as much, or more, energy (resources) than it requires to produce recreation and leisure service. The transformation of resources and information into programs and services enables a system to sustain its operations as long as its programs and services are needed or desired. Citizen involvement and synergetic programming methods, and new sources of resources and ideas, enable a system to sustain itself.

4. *Feedback.* Feedback is the steady flow of information that is produced as a response to a system's output or output by its subsystems. It is the process by which a system maintains equilibrium, a homeostatic process that serves to regulate, control, and immediately adjust a system's operations. Feedback is illustrated by Figure 4.1. It provides a system with a method of evaluating the effectiveness of its operations and output.

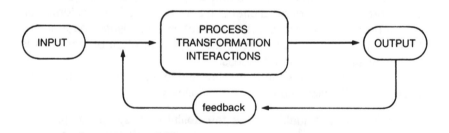

FIGURE 4.1 *Basic systems feedback.*

5. *System environment.* For a given system, the environment is a set of elements in which a change in any one will affect a change in the system and, likewise, the system will produce changes in the environment in which it coexists. The social, economic, political, educational, commercial, industrial, and natural environments affect the quality and quantity of recreation and leisure services, and

these services affect the quality of the environment by serving to enrich the quality of life. Figure 4.2 depicts a recreation and leisure-service system interfacing with other systems in the social and physical environment.

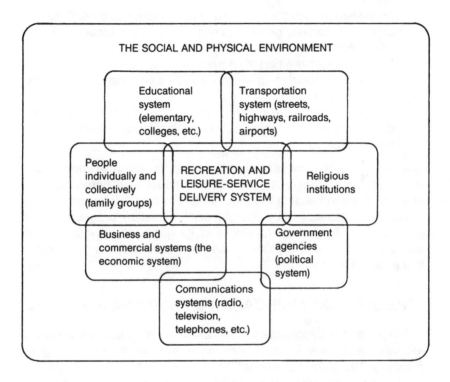

FIGURE 4.2   *Recreation and leisure - service systems environments.*

SYSTEMS EFFECTIVENESS

A system is considered to be effective when the people who enforce its management, planning, and technical and decision-making functions understand its purpose and contribute their individual efforts to the organization's success. Hopeman proposed that there are several characteristics of a system that can be observed in its design; each contributes to its effectiveness.[2] They include the following:

1. The overall objectives are meaningful.
2. Specialized operating and managerial decisional units interrelate to achieve objectives. These units may be represented by physical

flow patterns of materials, personnel, money, machines, and communications.

3. It contains a series of *(a)* inputs, *(b)* processes whereby value is added to input, and *(c)* outputs that relate to the fulfillment of overall objectives.

4. The system includes a set of external environmental relationships, such as customers, general public, government, labor, suppliers, and stockholders.

5. The system itself is a part of an even larger system. For example, the management decision-making system is a subsystem of the larger organizational system.

6. There is a need for evaluation and control. Since actual performance of the system may not meet objectives, corrective action may be required.

A system's effectiveness is improved when its personnel know how to use it. Efficient systems provide orientations for their personnel, thus enabling them to become more competent in the performance of their duties and responsibilities. A system's orientation program should provide for a better understanding of its goals, objectives, policies, procedures, rules and regulations, and the relationships and processes that enable it to operate.

THE SYSTEMS APPROACH TO PROGRAM PLANNING

The process of transforming needs and resources into recreation and leisure opportunities is an application of systems theory to program planning. The planning process involves a number of expected and predictable interactions that occur between the programmer (recreation specialist or planner), the subsystems, and the system's environments. The interactions occur whether a planner uses the systems approach or any other program-planning process. Interactions are natural occurrences involved in planning recreation activities designed to be responsive to people's needs.

Recreation and leisure-service systems exist to provide opportunities for people to engage individually and collectively in recreation behavior. The systems approach to planning concentrates on people and their needs. It seeks to provide opportunities that *(a)* satisfy people's recreation needs, *(b)* promote experiences that contribute to personal growth and development or the discovery of one's potential, and *(c)* that enrich the quality of life.

The planning process is initiated in response to recreation needs by administrative or policy-making board directive. It can also be initiated by a programmer on receipt of needs data, recreation resources, or feedback. It is a continuous process that perpetuates itself as long as recreation and leisure services are wanted or needed in any given environment. The planning process, having the characteristics of a system, can be initiated spontaneously to create new or needed programs as a by-product of its interactions. Conceptually, this occurs in the planning of a specific activity and, in the process, the programmer discovers the need and the resources to produce the activity and also for producing other needed recreation activities.

In practice, a recreation professional may be responsible for planning:

1. Comprehensive programs for a community or agency.
2. Programs for a target population, for example, an age group, men, women, special populations, employee groups, or families.
3. Facilities, for example, playgrounds, sports complexes, community centers, swim centers, or camps.
4. Programs by discipline or profession, for example, art, dance, dramatics, outdoor, or social recreation.
5. A program for a club or special-interest group.
6. An educational experience or special event.
7. A program for therapeutic purposes.

The following sequential systems procedures represent a synthesis of effective and efficient program-planning processes that are applicable to any recreation program-planning task.

DEFINITION OF THE SYSTEM'S PURPOSE

The first phase of the planning process involves the programmer becoming familiar with the system's goals and objectives. This procedure may also include an analysis of *(a)* administrative policy, *(b)* procedures, *(c)* principles of recreation and programming, *(d)* legal statutes, *(e)* rules and regulations, and *(f)* administrative directives or interpretations related to a system's mission.

Goals and objectives reveal a system's general purpose or intent, and serve as the basis for planning activities and delivering services. They specify the types of opportunities to be provided and the conditions for providing them, and provide the criteria for decision making and evaluating results. Goals and objectives provide an indication of expected results and serve as guidelines for developing program objectives and activities.

The specific goals accomplished by the programmer in the first phase of the systems approach to programming should include the following:

1. A review of the system's goals and objectives.

2. A clarification of the system's general purpose, objectives, policies, and procedures.
3. Specification of the system's general program intent, activities, and program scope.
4. Establishment of the criteria for decision making and for evaluating all aspects of the system's program-planning process and its general operations.

The programmer derives authority to initiate the program-planning process from the system's goals and objectives through administrative or policy-making board directive.

NEEDS ASSESSMENT

The second interdependent phase of the systems approach to programming is a twofold process in which recreation needs and resources are identified. The information decision-making and economic-technical subsystems processes are used to select appropriate procedures for identifying needs in the social environment and resources in the socio-physical environment. The needs assessment generally precedes the identification of resources.

The needs-assessment process justifies the system's existence by identifying and documenting recreation need and demand. Demographic data are used as a basis for needs assessment, and information about people's attitudes, values, interests, abilities, activities, and experiences is collected. The needs assessment enables the programmer to determine the type of activity experiences that will satisfy recreation needs and when, where, and how appropriate activities can be provided. The process identifies, collects, classifies, and analyzes recreation needs and demands to provide a database for selecting appropriate activities and for developing program objectives. The following research techniques may be used to assess needs:

1. Community input procedures, personal requests, and interviews using Q-sort or Delphi techniques to evaluate the data.
2. Observation and evaluation of recreation behavior.
3. Observation of recreation areas and facilities.
4. Surveys and interest inventories utilizing questionnaires or checklists.
5. Case studies.

The second phase identifies the social, fiscal, and physical resource base that is used to support the system and recreation activities. The following information is gathered:

1. *Human resources.* Information pertaining to people's abilities, interests, and experiences is obtained to support the system, and activities, support group's volunteers, and technical assistance personnel are identified.
2. *Financial resources.* The tax base is evaluated, the budget is reviewed, and the state of the economy and discretionary spending are analyzed.
3. *Support resources.* The sources of supplies, equipment, and materials are identified.
4. *Physical resources.* Existing recreation areas and facilities, areas and facilities with potential for recreation use, and existing programs and services are identified and classified for future reference and use.

Identification of recreation needs, demands, and resources provides the programmer with a sound base for establishing program priorities and for planning appropriate, responsive, and feasible activity opportunities. The system for comprehensive planning initiates a major needs-assessment project on an annual or semiannual basis. This establishes a database for program planning during a specified period and eliminates the process when planning to meet specific needs. A minor needs assessment can be conducted for each activity requested or suggested by citizen input to a system if there are insufficient data to support or deny its planning. Figure 4.3 illustrates the needs-assessment procedure. The system interacts with both the social and physical environment to assess needs and resources, and receives input from any source at any time that it is operational.

DEVELOPMENT OF PROGRAM OBJECTIVES.

The third phase of the system's interdependent approach to program planning is the development of program objectives. In this phase, the programmer interacts with and uses the subsystems to develop concise and specific statements of program purpose and intent. Program objectives specify in advance the goals to be attained, needs to be satisfied, activities to be provided, and resources to be used, and are used as the criteria for qualitative and quantitative evaluations. They establish a method of maintaining accountability in relation to the achievement of goals, the satisfaction of needs, and the use of resources. Program objectives specify:

1. The population to be served by age, sex, or other demographic characteristics, and the specific needs to be satisfied.

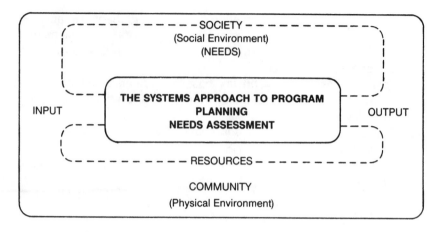

FIGURE 4.3 *Needs-assessment procedure, external interactions with environments.*

2. The activities or services to be provided by program classification and expected results.
3. The schedule (time, place, date) and duration of an activity or service, and the priority for promoting it.
4. The areas or facilities to be used, and the conditions for using them.
5. The leadership to be provided (if any); the materials, supplies, and equipment required; procedures for providing or conducting an activity; the program format; and the source of fiscal support (a free or fee-type activity).

Objectives provide specific directions for achieving results related to a system's goals and participants' needs. The program objectives identify the general characteristics of the program and the activities to be provided in specific situations.

ACTIVITY AND COST ANALYSIS

The fourth phase of the systems approach to program planning is the activity and cost-benefit analysis. The information-decision making and economic-technical subsystems are utilized by the programmer to determine if the selected activites will contribute to the attainment of program objectives and if they are economically feasible to produce. "Activity analysis is a procedure for breaking down and examining an activity to find inherent characteristics that contribute to program objectives."[3] The results promoted by an activity and the requirement for producing it are identified by these procedures. The cost-benefit analysis determines if the benefits derived from an activity warrant the cost of producing it. Activity and cost analysis are procedures for determining, in advance, the benefits inherent in any activity specified by the program objectives. The procedure provides information for making objective decisions in the process of developing activity opportunities related to the attainment of a system's goals and objectives.

OPERATIONAL PLANNING

The fifth phase of the systems approach to program planning involves all subsystems in the development of plans to transform program objectives into actual activities. The requirements for producing the activities determined to be feasible by the activity analysis are listed. The leadership, supplies, equipment, areas, and facilities required to produce an activity are listed on a program evaluation review technique flowchart. A time line is established to finalize the organization of the plans for securing the allocation of the required resources to conduct the activity. Procedures for promoting, registering participants, and conducting activities are planned, and then the administrator authorizes the implementation of the planned activity or programs.

PROMOTION AND IMPLEMENTATION.

The sixth phase involves all subsystems in the output of program activities. Promotional strategies are used to inform and invite participation and complete registration. The implementation of opportunities for people to engage in recreation behavior accomplishes the system's primary goal.

FEEDBACK AND CONTINUOUS EVALUATION.

The final phase is feedback and evaluation. All subsystems are involved in the evaluation of external and internal feedback.

External feedback occurs as a result of systems output and provides the information used for the summative evaluation of its overall effectiveness by comparing results with program objectives. It indicates whether a system's output has successfully met the needs and interests of people or what corrective measures are required. It also provides information for increasing a program's effectiveness and for redefining priorities.

Internal feedback occurs continuously between the system's subsystems in each of the sequential planning phases. It provides information for the formulative evaluation that controls and coordinates the interactions inherent in the program-planning process. Internal feedback confirms or provides information that increases a system's efficiency and effectiveness.

Feedback is continuously compared with goals and objectives to ensure that systematically developed plans and programs effectively meet the needs of people and that resources are used efficiently.

SUMMARY

Recreation program planning involves and consists of many functions that are characteristic of a system. Systems theory explains the patterned interactive processes that involve the interdependent and interrelated functions of an organization's component parts involved in planning. Systems are organizations that use the specialized abilities of their component parts to achieve specific ends. A system's operations consist of a series of inputs, processes, and outputs. Recreation program planning, likewise, consists of procedures that rely on open and continuous (input) of information and resources to plan and organize (process) and implement (output) recreation opportunities for people. The progressive series of interdependent and interrelated interactions involved in planning recreation activities and programs is a flexible and responsive decision-making process. The systems approach to recreation programming utilizes the system's goals and objectives as the criteria for making decisions related to providing opportunities that effectively and efficiently use available resources.

ENDNOTES

1. Owen, J. L., Page, P. A., and Zimmerman, G. (1975). Communications in organizations. St. Paul, MN: West Publishing Company.
2. Hopeman, R. J. (1969). Systems analysis and operations management. Columbus, OH: Charles E. Merrill Publishing Company.
3. Gunn, S. L. and Peterson, C. A. (1982), Therapeutic recreation program design (p. 156). Englewood Cliffs, NJ: Prentice Hall, Inc.

5

NEEDS ASSESSMENT

The systems approach to recreation program planning involves identifying people's needs and then organizing the resources necessary to produce activity opportunities that satisfy these needs. The planning process consists of seven sequential phases; the examination of the system's goals and objectives to determine its basic purpose is the first. The second phase of the systems approach to recreation program planning is the needs assessment. In practice, needs assessment is a dual-purpose process of identifying needs and resources. This chapter will concentrate on the needs assessment process; and procedures for identifying recreation resources are discussed in chapter 6.

The inherent effectiveness of the systems approach is that it seeks and uses the input of needs data and resources in the planning and organization of recreation activities. The needs-assessment procedure enhances the planning process by providing the programmer with information related to people's needs. Activities that are related to people's needs are then planned. The importance of recreation need was revealed by analyzing the operations of recreation and leisure-service systems. The analysis revealed the following:

1. Recreation and leisure services are justified as permanent and legitimate functions of public, private, and commercial agencies on the basis of needs.
2. Resources for their operations are allocated on the basis of need.
3. Programs, services, and facilities are planned on the basis of need.

The systems approach to recreation programming improves on other planning methods by concentrating on a system's goals and objectives and people's needs to plan and produce activity opportunities. In this chapter, the concept of recreation need is discussed, the ocnditions that promote needs are examined, and indicators of need and sources of data for the needs assessment are reviewed. Procedures for identifying individual and community needs are also examined.

RECREATION NEED

The concept of recreation need was discussed by Mercer, who identified four types of need for planning purposes.[1] He presented the concepts of normative, felt, expressed, and comparative needs.

1. Normative needs are conceived of as basic needs for which there are recreation planning standards established by experts in various fields associated with recreation and leisure services. Opportunities provided for people to engage in physical, creative, cultured, and other activities are considered to be based on normative needs.
2. Felt needs are basic drives that impel an individual to act to satisfy a particular need.
3. Expressed needs are simply felt needs put into action or request for appropriate opportunities to satisfy a felt need.
4. Comparative needs are the actual discrepancies that exist in what is available in terms of quality and quantity in one place and another or for one group and another.

The concept of recreation need requires further definition to allow planners to identify needs for program-planning purposes.

Psychologists have suggested that a need is a state of disequilibrium within the biophysical, social, and psychological aspects of a person's being. Disequilibrium produces stress or tension within the organism that compels that person to act to reduce stress or tension, attaining a state of equilibrium. Horrocks explained that stress releases a drive within the organism that is directly proportional to the persistence or importance of the need.[2] The action directed at reducing stress is behavior. We understand that needs are the foundations of all human behavior and that humans learn different patterns of behavior through social interaction. We further understand that individuals differ in their methods of satisfying needs and that they interact with others to satisfy other needs. Human behavior is characterized as complex; it is a result of activity directed at meeting a need. Methods of satisfying needs are subject to change in relation to situational demand and learning. Human need is the basis of recreation behavior and recreation serves to satisfy needs that originate on a hierarchy of needs, for example, Maslow's and a trilateral continuum.[3] The continuum consists of intrinsic and extrinsic drives, learned behavior and situational demands, and environmental factors and opportunities. (See Figure 5.1)

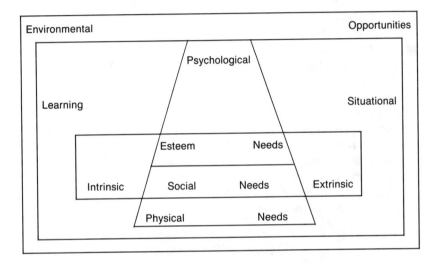

FIGURE 5.1   *Maslow's hierarchy of needs and the trilateral continuum of need
-drives.*

We have not discovered exactly where recreation need originates in this matrix of human behavior. However, we infer that it occurs as a synthesis of hierarchical needs and lateral drives. Research indicates that recreation experiences satisfy a person's interdependent and interrelated biophysical, social, and psychological needs. Gray's defin- ition of recreation suggests that there are aspects of the experience that satisfy various categorical needs which, for our purposes, can be considered normative.[4] Horrocks[2] suggested that inference of need can be made by using one of the following methods:

1.   From a series of observations
2.   From an analysis of case studies or records
3.   From free responses to broad questions
4.   From responses to a problem inventory or list

The methods suggested by Horrocks for making inferences require a programmer to use a systematic process to analyze behavior. The twelve psychological needs identified by Horrocks, and the fourteen recreation behaviors listed by Murphy, Williams, Niepoth, and Brown[5] in chapter 2 provide one approach to identifying needs from a psychological perspective. For example, socializing behavior relates to most recreation experiences because there are numerous social encounters involved when a person engages in any activity. The individual who engages in a dual, group, class, or team activity is afforded an opportunity to satisfy such psychological needs as acceptance, approval, belonging, conformity, and recognition. The same conceptual relationships can be inferred between physiological and social needs and other recreation behaviors. Inference of recreation need is based on an understanding that all humans have similar needs.

Recreation is pursued with intensity and the situations that precede involvement provide an indication of need. The societal conditions or situations that precede recreation behavior provide the programmer with objective data for determing the recreation need. Social indicators and demographic data provide the base for objectively determining the scope and depth of recreation need, interests, and expectation.

SOCIAL INDICATORS

Social indicators, Neuliner concluded, are "the monitoring tools of social progress."[6] They are a longitudinal measurement of socially relevant variables in which change occurs over a period of time in the general state of human welfare. Social indicators reveal, more directly than do demographic data, the extraneous pressures that create recreation needs as they provide insight into the trends and the general direction in which society is moving.

Modern America is characterized as a democratic, technically advanced, internationally involved, informed, and changing multi-cultured society. Social scientists are constantly monitoring all aspects of life to systematically analyze the effects of change and progress on the general quality of life. Social indicators reveal that we live in a highly competitive and progressive society that is densely populated in its metropolitan areas, and that pollution adversely affects all living things. There is evidence that change and progress are creating new jobs, new technology, and new economic roles for women and minorities. There is renewed emphasis on quality education and belief in the American tradition that there is equal access to opportunity for all.

In determining need, the recreation programmer must examine neutral and negative trends to plan adequate programs. Characterizations of the workplace, the dissolution of the family, increasing numbers of unattended children (latch key), unemployment, and the crime rate are social indicators that reveal needs. The analysis of economic indicators reveals trends that generally affect recreation demand. Characterizations of the workplace suggest that work is no longer the center of a person's identity and that recreation activities are becoming increasingly more important aspects of our lives. Leisure spending is another trend revealed by social indicators. Social trends and issues, such as the temporary nature of our relationships and demands on our time, are subject to analysis. Nearly twenty-five years ago, DeGrazia said that our lives are controlled by the clock.[7] We eat, sleep, work, go to school, and live by the clock, and there is never enough time. Conditions affecting time have not changed in relation to our social and economic obligations in the past quarter of a century and we may be still losing control of our time. Time, not necessarily leisure, is essential for the production and consumption of recreation opportunities.

Social indicators provide the programmer with insight into the normative patterns of people's lifestyles. They reveal data related to the types of recreation activities that may be appropriate to reduce the stress created and sustained by the complex nature of modern society.

DEMOGRAPHIC DATA

Demographic data represent the classification of people by age, sex, height, weight, race, color, ethnic origin, and other personal characteristics. In the needs-assessment process, demographic data are used to define the subjects of a descriptive research project. This process is not just concerned with determining how many people there are, the population density, and composition. It seeks to determine:

1. The place of residence
2. The level of educational attainment
3. Occupation and income level
4. Information pertaining to access and personal mobility.

These data are then used to project needs based upon a sampling of the general population. Descriptive research procedures, "the accumulation of a database that is solely descriptive,"[8] are used to identify and define needs for recreation and leisure experiences. The Census

Bureau, local planning commissions, chambers of commerce, boards of education, and sometimes the local telephone company are sources of demographic data.

In planning a recreation activity, demographic data are used to project the actual numbers of people who must be included in a representative sample. The programmer's understanding of recreation needs and social indicators provide, with demographical data, a base for an objective and subjective, and quantitative and qualitative, analysis of needs data.

NEEDS ASSESSMENT

Needs assessment is a descriptive research procedure used to identify and define recreation need, and to determine the discrepancies that exist between needs and opportunities. The process consists of seven steps.

DEFINING RECREATION NEED

Recreation is a special kind of human behavior that evolves from a deficiency in any aspect of a person's being. In the context of the needs assessment for planning purposes, a need is defined as a deficiency that activates an inherent drive within an individual. It is a cognitive function, a response to a situation that is appropriate for an expression of the self, and which satisfies a deficiency. Generally, recreation needs are acquired and lead one to experiences that are positive and highly desirable as they serve to reinforce a sense of personal well-being. Recreation needs are best explained in terms of human behavior; therefore, at this time a programmer can only infer that there are recreation needs.

Needs assessment is a process of making inferences—for this purpose, recreation needs are classified as felt, expressed, normative, and comparative. They originate from the cognitive, affective, and psychomotor domains of human behavior and persist throughout all stages of human development. Recreation needs for assessment purposes are best described as activities in the functional categories in which most recreation endeavors occur. The categories are as follows:

1. *Creative:* all arts, crafts, forms of dance, drama, music, and literary pursuits.
2. *Cultural:* ethnic and folk celebrations, folk music, dance, classical art, music, and other performances.

3. *Educational or literary:* all recreation classes, opportunities for vicarious experiences, personal development, contemplation, and so forth.
4. *Outdoor or environmental:* camping, hiking, fishing, adventure and risk activities, vehicular activities, and pursuits involving nature.
5. *Physical:* fitness and movement-type activities, aquatics, competitive athletics and sports, games, relaxation, and physical refreshment.
6. *Services:* civic projects, volunteering, and other community services-type activities.
7. *Social and symbolic endeavors:* club or group activities, visiting with friends, and other activities promoting human interactions of a social nature.

IDENTIFYING THE STUDY SUBJECTS

The subjects are selected as individuals, groups, neighborhoods, and the community at large to determine recreation needs, wants, and desires. Demographical data are examined to randomly select a sample that is representative of the community at large or any subgroup considered to have special recreations needs.

COLLECTING THE DATA

There are several alternative methods to consider for collecting data.

1. The personal interview, a time-consuming and lengthy process, is normally a reliable technique. Reliable inferences can be made from the database collected. This is a very appropriate method of assessing the needs of the disabled and special populations.
2. Making personal observations is a subjective approach, unless definitive descriptive criteria are developed to evaluate observed behavior.
3. Analyzing case studies is another alternative method.
4. A person can also administer interests inventories, checklists, and questionnaires to groups, organizations, and the community at large.
5. Program records and evaluations can be used to collect data.
6. Community involvement input techniques have proved to be a reliable source of needs data when the group is representative of the community at large.

Checklists administered to groups at meetings and structured to seek specific information provide a reliable source and method of collecting all types of data. Questionnaires mailed to all addresses or selected groups of people are far more difficult to use for needs-assessment purposes. People generally do not respond to questionnaires and limited responses may provide invalid findings or results.

SELECTING A REPRESENTATIVE POPULATION SAMPLE

In developing a recreation profile for a group or community, a stratified random sample is recommended to ensure that a representative sample of the population is included in the study. Procedures for selecting sample groups are explained in most introductory education or psychology texts.

SELECTING OR DESIGNING THE ASSESSMENT TOOL

A few tools are commercially available. If costs are prohibitive or a commercial instrument is not adaptable for local use, one can be developed by consulting Theobald, *Evaluation of Recreation and Parks Programs,* selected Therapeutic recreation and Introduction to Research texts.[9] Farrell and Lundegren describe five types of needs assessment: activity interests or preference, general descriptive data profiling participants, evaluations of programs and services, the identification of nonusers, and assessment of attitudes about proposed programs and services.[10] The systems approach to program planning utilizes the needs-assessment process in the formulation of a program and descriptive data, activity preference, or interests; the attitudes of participants and nonparticipants are required for effective planning. Checklists, questionnaires, and other needs-assessment instruments should provide the programmer with the following:

1. A discrete and descriptive profile of the subjects. These data should consist of name (if appropriate), age, sex, marital status, number of dependents, area of residence, occupation, income level, and means or mode of transportation.
2. A listing of the subjects activity interests or preferences arranged in functional program categories. This section should be preceded by instructions for completing the form and answering any questions.
3. An assessment of attitudes about programs and services. This should be on a Likert scale and include (SA) strongly agree, (A) agree, (N) neutral, (D) disagree, (SD) strongly disagree, and (N/A) not applicable.

The checklist, Figure 5.2, identifies recreation interests, which are an indication of preference or need. The checklist was developed for use during a personal interview and has been used with groups and

NAME _____ AGE _____, M _____, F _____, HEALTH STATUS _____

ADDRESS _____ ZIP CODE _____, PHONE NO. _____, MARITAL STATUS _____

NO. DEPENDENTS _____, INCOME _____, OCCUPATION _____, MEANS OF TRANSPORTATION _____

RECREATION ACTIVITIES

PROGRAM FORMAT	ARTS & CRAFTS	DANCE	DRAMA	MUSIC	OUTDOOR	SPORTS	SOCIAL/SERVICE
SPECIAL EVENTS Exhibitions Mass Activity Performances Social Events	Arts & Crafts Shows Hobby Shows Exhibitions	Contest Exhibitions Performances	Ceremonies Productions Community Theatrical	Performing Individual Group Festivals	Trips & Outings Demonstrations	All Sports Tournaments Fun Runs Track Meets Pro-Ams Rodeos	Banquets Award Ceremonies Fund Raisers Carnivals
COMPETITIVE ACTIVITIES Tournaments Contest Leagues Playdays	Drawing Painting Photo Contents etc.	Contest Marathon	Debate Talent Shows	Vocal Band Talent Shows Creative Contests	Hang Gliding Winter Sports Fishing Boating	Single Double Elimination Tourney and Leagues All Sports	Fund Raising Activities Fun Runs Pro Amateur Events
CLASSES/CLINICS Educational Activities Workshops Skill Development	Candle Making Leather Craft Wood & Ceramics Projects Sculpture	Folk Ballet Social Ethnic Disco	Puppetry Mime Combined	Vocal Instrumental Appreciation	Nature Outdoor Living Living Skills	Instruction In all Sports	Income Tax Preparation
CLUBS Associative Affiliate	Photo Clubs etc.	Square Dance	Drama Clubs	Glee Clubs	Ski Clubs	Golf, Tennis Clubs	Service Clubs
OPEN ACTIVITIES Drop In Casual Partici- pation, Self-Directed	Appreciation Behaviors Spontaneous Activities	Observations Open Dancing	Spectator Activity	Listening	Camping Zoos Aboreturns Gardening	Free Play	Volunteering

Specific Activities should be substituted for the general activities listed above.

FIGURE 5.2 Individual recreation needs assessment checklist.

Source: Adapted from Murphy, Farrell and Lundegren.

organizations. It is limited to preference for activity and does not account for skill or ability level or for personal access or mobility. The programmer can add an additional dimension to any assessment instrument to determine the ability or skill level of the participants. Lynn Jamison presented a paper, "The Sports Hierarchy," which outlined the various skill and ability levels associated with sports participation.[11] The following ability-skill levels were originally identified by Richard Mull at Indiana University and they ascend a hierarchy from the beginner-instructional level to higher levels of ability or skill. Figure 5.3 illustrates the skill-ability levels associated with sports participation, a similar scale is recommended for other recreation activities.

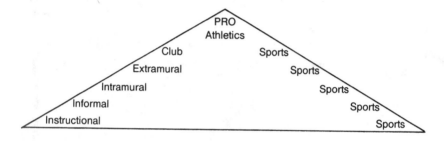

FIGURE 5.3 *Sports hierarchy.*

Source: Used by permission of Richard Mull, Indiana University.

The skill or ability level for any functional category of a recreation program can be determined by activity analysis or a program classification system. The American Red Cross swimming classification system—beginner, advanced beginner, intermediate, swimmer, and advanced swimmer—are appropriate for indicating the level of recreation skill or ability, and fit into the scheme of a five-point rating scale (Likert) previously suggested for assessing attitudes.

COLLECTING, CLASSIFYING, ANALYZING, AND INTERPRETING THE DATA

This step is self-explanatory. The instrument adopted or developed for the assessment should enable the programmer to identify participants and nonparticipants by age, sex, activity preference, interests, and ability. The data should be arranged so that they can be evaluated objectively and subjectively, and quantitatively and qualitatively. Russell, an advocate of the community leadership involvement, input method of program planning, suggests that the Nominal Group Process (NGP) technique is a means of determining "what are the most pressing recreational needs of the community."[12] NGP is a procedure that can be used to assess needs during group meetings. All group participants respond to a specific question and all answers to a question are recorded. Then there is a round-robin discussion of each response. The large group is then divided into small groups of not more than ten members each. The small groups discuss all responses, rank-order each, and then report to the large group, where the small group rankings are tallied to represent the consensus of the large group. The NGP technique and other participatory decision-making procedures generally require that small-group leaders or facilitators have some knowledge of group evaluative procedures. This technique can be used to classify, analyze, and interpret data.

REPORTING OR USING THE DATA FOR PLANNING PURPOSES

The needs-assessment process is too demanding for a programmer to go through the procedure and then not use the information to plan or revise recreation programs. Using the information obtained, the programmer can match participant wants, needs, interests, and abilities with opportunities that are specifically planned for the participants. The recreation experience is enhanced when activities are scheduled at appropriate times and when they are planned at various skill or ability levels of the participants. Participant frustrations are also reduced when there are alternative levels for involvement provided.

Recreation preferences or interests, and inferred need, provide a base for developing all types of programs; including classes, clinics, club or special-interest groups, leagues and tournaments, special events, social recreation, outreach programs, and open or free-play activities.

COMMUNITY NEEDS

The procedures used to determine the recreation needs of individuals and groups provide the data that are used to develop a community's or an agency's needs profile. Generally, all recreation and leisure-service organizations evaluate their programs, services, and facilities prior to the preparation of their budgets. Self-studies are used to determine needs for programs, services, and facilities, and program effectiveness. Comparative needs provide the database for master planning, environmental impact analysis, redevelopment plans, and participation in many grant programs. They also provide the basis for advanced planning and the distribution of recreation services. The procedures used to determine needs for activity opportunities provide the information required to determine these needs and to predict future needs.

SUMMARY

Needs assessment in the program-planning process is a procedure used to identify recreation needs. Systems programmers use needs as a basis for planning responsive programs, services, and facilities. A recreation need, however, is an acquired need and for program-planning purposes recreation needs are inferred. Inferred need for recreation is a concept based on the psychological perspective of need. Recreation need evolves from the intrinsic and extrinsic drives originating from biological and socio-psychological disequilibrium within an organism. Social indicators reveal that contemporary living conditions constantly sustain situations that cause stress and tension within individuals and create recreation needs.

Demographical data are used to identify the subjects of the needs assessment, and descriptive research procedures are utilized to complete the study. The concept of recreation need is verified when people, individually and collectively, engage in planned programs and use recreation services and facilities.

The objective and systematic use of quantitative and qualitative research procedures for needs-assessment purposes in the 1980s provides information for planning relevant and responsive programs, services, and facilities. The procedures used to assess recreation needs should be compatible with existing computer programs for data processing purposes to eliminate delays in the program planning process.

ENDNOTES

1.   Mercer, D. (1973, Winter). The concept of recreation need, *Journal of Leisure Research, 5* (1), 37-47.
2.   Horrocks, J. E. (1962). *The psychology of adolescence,* (pp. 502-507). Boston: Houghton Mifflin Company.
3.   Maslow, A. (1966). In P. Hersey & K. H. Blanchard (Eds.), *Management of Organizational Behavior* (3rd ed., Englewood Cliffs, NJ: Prentice Hall, Inc. p. 18).
4.   Gray, D. E. (1971, December 12). *Recreation: An interpretation* (Summary of Research Finding). Long Beach, CA: California State University.
5.   Murphy, J. F., Williams, J. G., Niepoth, E. W., & Brown, P. D. (1972). *Leisure service delivery system* (p. 73). Philadelphia: Lea & Febiger.

6. Neuliner, J. (1981). *To leisure: An introduction* (p. 87). Boston: Allyn & Bacon.
7. DeGrazia, S. (1962). *Of time, work and leisure.* New York: Twentieth Century Fund.
8. Isaaz, S., & Michael, W. B. (1971). *Handbook in research and evaluation* (p. 18). San Diego, CA: Edits Publishing.
9. Theobald, W. F. (1979). *Evaluation of recreation and park programs.* New York: John Wiley and Sons.
10. Farrell, P., & Lundegren, H. M. *The process of recreation programming* (pp. 81-100). New York: John Wiley and Sons.
11. Jamison, L. (1981, November). *Sports heirarchy.* Paper presented at the educators workshop, California Society of Park and Recreation Educators, Alisoimeir, CA.
12. Russell, R. (1982). *Planning programs in recreation* (pp. 92-95). St. Louis: C. V. Mosby.

6

COMMUNITY RESOURCES

The needs-assessment process provides the programmer with data pertaining to recreation needs. The data collected by the assessment process are evaluated and the needs that are consistent with the system's purpose are acted upon. The programmer begins to organize the resources necessary to produce recreation activities that are related to and responsive to the recreation needs of the community at large.

In the second phase of the assessment process, the resources that are necessary to organize and produce recreation programs and services, and operate facilities, are identified. Chubb and Chubb identified twenty-three public, private, and commercial providers of organized recreation, leisure, and cultural programs.[1] The decision to provide any one program is primarily contingent upon the availability of resources. The primary types of resources required to produce recreation and leisure services are human, fiscal, and physical. Human resources are the personnel who manage and operate recreation and leisure-service organizations. Fiscal or financial resources are required to meet all financial obligations of an organization. Physical resources are buildings, equipment, and the area required to promote, conduct, and maintain recreation and leisure services.

HUMAN RESOURCES

The efficient operation of any organization is dependent upon the effectiveness of its personnel. Professional leaders are responsible for planning and organizing a variety of recreation and leisure-service programs that promote human development and personal satisfaction. Additional leadership is required to conduct many of the activities so that the program's goals and objectives are attainable. The programmer is required to identify personnel in the community at large to conduct the activities and supervise the facilities used for recreation purposes.

Individuals with leadership potential, unique skills, and abilities are identified through personal contacts, advertising, and public relations. Contact with interest groups, participants, colleges and universities, volunteer service organizations, civic and service organizations, and other human service agencies enable the programmer to develop a reference file for maintaining the names, addresses, telephone numbers, and skills and interests of persons who are available to provide program leadership on a full-time, part-time, or voluntary basis. Individuals can often be identified through the needs-assessment process or during program registration. Identifying personnel and providing responsible leadership, instruction, or supervision reduces the risks—personal and legal—that are involved in recreation programming.

FINANCIAL RESOURCES

The programmer is required to identify the source of the financial resources used to support organized programs sponsored by an agency. Public, private, and commercial recreation and leisure-service organizations receive their fiscal support from different sources. Public agencies are generally supported by tax revenue; private and voluntary organizations rely on memberships, endowments, fund raising, contributions, and donations. Commercial recreation programs are sustained by the profits earned.

Needs-assessment data, demographical information, and social indicators pertaining to the economy are reviewed to identify additional sources or alternative methods of supporting recreation activities. The needs-assessment process can be used to identify special-interest groups with the leadership and financial ability to sustain an activity initially sponsored by an agency. Interest groups can be organized as nonprofit organizations to provide activities. Corporate sponsors have been identified to sponsor activities in some communities and sports associations. For example, the United States Tennis Association conducts tournaments and clinics in cooperation with recreation and leisure-service agencies. In cooperation with public park and recreation departments, Coca Cola, Hershey's candy, and the Atlantic Richfield Company sponsor local, state, regional, and national competitions.

Knowledge of the community enables the programmer to identify the leaders of the chamber of commerce, civic, and service organizations who are supportive of recreation and leisure services. Identifying supportive community leaders enables a programmer to establish a local park and recreation foundation or initiate a gifts catalog program. Deppe cites, under "other sources of revenue," two additional alternatives—grants from foundations and philanthropic organizations, and "Partnerships for People."[2]

Federal programs that provide financial aid for local park and recreation programs are generally limited to planning and development, needs assessment, the acquisition of land, and the development of areas and facilities. Eligibility for participating in federal matching grant programs is generally based upon need, economic and physical distress, and the relative quality and condition of the local park and recreation system. Normally, federal grant funds are not used to support activity programs.

Funds to support local activities above and beyond the allocated budget come from program fees and charges. Edginton and Williams[3] and Deppe[2] identify seven alternative revenue sources:

1. Entrance fees.
2. Admission fees.
3. Rental fees.
4. User fees.
5. Sales revenue.
6. License and permit fees.
7. Special-service fees.

A number of organizations have adopted policies that in effect state that recreation activities are to be supported by those who participate, rather than the public at large. Information obtained by the needs assessment provides the programmer with information for determining which of the needed activities can be offered as self-sustaining activities and which must be fully or partially supported by the agency.

The programmer's knowledge of local economic conditions enables him or her to identify those participants who are willing to pay for services and how much they are willing to pay. Howard and Crompton discussed five strategies for setting up a fees-and-charges schedule.[4] Two are revenue-producing strategies—the going rate and demand-oriented pricing. Verifying recreation demand through the needs-assessment process, the programmer can recommend that the going rate be charged for a recreation service. The going rate is essentially what people are willing to pay and others are charging. Fees that are charged for recreation services generally recover a portion or the full cost of providing an activity for a specified period. The total cost of producing an activity plus a small profit is recommended when participants can afford the extra tariff. Profits from these activities are used to support non-revenue-producing activities.

PHYSICAL RESOURCES

The needs-assessment process identifies the activities in which people will participate and determines, through the resource identification phase, if there are resources to conduct recreation and leisure activities. The programmer is responsible for identifying every possible area and facility within a system's service area that can be used for programming purposes. Identifying and determining which areas and facilities can be used to conduct activities, disseminate information, and store equipment is a prerequisite to scheduling activities. Determining the carrying capacity (number of people a facility will accommodate) and which facilities can be used to conduct different activities enables the programmer to plan a comprehensive program. To schedule a comprehensive program and accommodate all participants requires access to a variety of areas and facilities. The programmer must identify and arrange to use public, private, and commercial recreation and leisure-service areas and facilities. These may include:

Adventure playgrounds	Athletic fields, courts and
Amphitheaters, auditoriums	stadiums
Bowling lanes	Bicycle and hiking trails
Camps	Community centers
Golf courses	Libraries
Lakes, ponds, rivers	Outdoor recreation areas
Harbors, marinas	Playgrounds
Parks and parkways	School buildings, grounds
Recreation centers	Swimming pools
Skating rinks (ice, roller)	Shopping malls

In addition to the facilities listed, churches, private clubs, meeting halls, dance halls and studios, health and fitness centers, theaters, and convention centers are used or can be used for recreation programs. Sports arenas, game rooms, racquetball and tennis clubs, hotel and motel meeting rooms, utility and railroad rights-of-way, airport approaches, and flood plains should be considered as potential areas and facilities.

In addition to identifying areas and facilities, the progammer should determine how accessible they are to the participants. Determining accessibility in advance facilitates the accommodation of the handicapped and other participants who may have limited mobility.

Identifying, inventorying, and securing the use of recreation and leisure-service facilities enables the programmer to plan activities that are related to the needs, interests, and abilities of the people expected to use them. Each May issue of *Parks and Recreation* consists of articles about innovative, unique, and creative use of areas and facilities.[5] Articles have reported about the innovative use of rooftops, parking lots, warehouses, abandoned businesses and houses, and play streets for programming purposes. Areas and facilities are essential for the delivery and distribution of services and to meet the demand for recreation and leisure opportunities. Public, private and, commercial agencies are now using a variety of nontraditional buildings and areas to provide programs.

OTHER RESOURCES

In the process of identifying a community's resources, the programmer can locate the businesses that can provide the supplies, equipment, and materials required to produce recreation activities. Businesses are identified to provide the sports equipment, art supplies, forms, and paper supplies necessary to produce programs and accomplish the administrative, personnel, financial, programming, and maintenance functions of an organization.

The programmer identifies where materials used for the construction, maintenance, and operations of a recreation and leisure-service system can be purchased in the community and which businesses are reliable sources. The businesses that can provide office furniture and equipment, automobiles, tractors and trucks, playground apparatus, baseball backstops, tennis nets, and hockey goals are identified as the programmer seeks contacts for the loan, lease, and purchase of recreation equipment.

Under the civil rights acts, the Transportation and Architectural Barriers Act, the Rehabilitation Act, and the Education of the Handicapped Act, federal legislation requires that public accommodations be accessible to all citizens. The programmer, in assessing a community's resources, should determine if participants have access to recreation areas and facilities. Public transportation and adequate parking in close proximity to areas and facilities are an asset that enables participation in planned programs.

In addition to determining accessibility, the programmer must provide the leadership to increase citizen awareness of the problems and needs of all citizens, and identify educators, physicians, newspaper editors, television commentators, and other citizens interested in recreation to assist in the promotion of the overall program. Educators and physicians who endorse the programs give them credibility and encourage people to participate. The news media, especially newspaper editors and radio and television personalities, are contacts (resources) for disseminating information and for establishing an effective public relations program. Public relations provide contact with the media to keep the public at large informed about all opportunities afforded the citizens.

SUMMARY

The identification of resources enables the programmer to evaluate the community's financial assets and determine what percentage of the total is available for the support of recreation and leisure services. Financial assets are the energy source that activates a delivery system and enables it to provide the personnel, supplies, equipment, areas, and facilities necessary to conduct recreation activities. An effective resource identification plan, combined with a good public relations program, enables a recreation and leisure-service system to generate support for all the programs, services, and facilities planned by a programmer. The primary accomplishments of the resource assessment process are the following:

1. Information is gained about existing recreation programs.
2. Information is obtained about the community's financial resources.
3. General information is gained about the community at large, the decision makers, the workers, and attitudes related to the general importance of recreation and the community's willingness to support programs.
4. Information is gained about existing facilities.
5. Information is obtained pertaining to the feasibility of producing activities.

The resource identification process provides the programmer with a basic knowledge of where to locate the resources needed to produce relevant and responsive recreation and leisure services.

ENDNOTES

1. Chubb, M. & Chubb, H. R. (1981). *One third of our time,* (pp. 634-635). New York: John Wiley and Sons.
2. Deppe, T. R. (1983). *Management strategies in financing parks and recreation,* (pp. 32-35). New York: John Wiley and Sons.
3. Edginton, C. R., & Williams, J. G. (1978). *Productive management of leisure service organizations,* (pp. 292-296). New York: John Wiley and Sons.
4. Howard, D. R. & Crompton, J. L. (1980). *Financing, managing and marketing recreation and park resources,* (pp. 428-446). Dubuque, IA: W. C. Brown Company.
5. *Parks and recreation,* (May issue, 1965 to present). Alexandria, VA: National Recreation and Parks Association.

7

PROGRAM OBJECTIVES

The third phase of the systems approach to recreation program planning involves the development of program objectives. A system's goals define its general purpose, and program objectives define the relationships between goals, people's needs, and how resources will be used to provide mutually responsive recreation opportunities. Program objectives serve to guide a system's efforts to attain its goals.

The needs-assessment and resource identification process (phase two) of the systems approach to programming provides the programmer with the information to plan activities that are related to recreation needs. Program objectives are planning statements that incorporate an understanding of the principles of recreation, a system's goals, people's needs, and how resources will be used to attain desired results. They are action statements that focus a programmer's effort toward the attainment of a system's goals by establishing a definite purpose for each activity, service, or facility provided. Objectives define the system's purpose, the activities to be provided, the people served, the expected outcomes, and the procedures for conducting activities. In developing program objectives, the programmer will generally identify the following:

1. The individuals or groups to be served.
2. The purpose of the activity or program in relation to the needs that the programmer seeks to satisfy.
3. The facility or setting in which the program or activity will be provided.

4. The schedule of events by program date, time, and duration.
5. The delivery or implementing procedure used to provide the program or activity.

Program objectives account for the leadership to be provided and the financial and other resources used in the production of a program, and provide the criteria used for program evaluation and accountability.

Recreation and leisure-service systems provide opportunities for people to engage in and enjoy recreation activities. In this chapter, the relationships between goals, principles, needs and resources, and planning activities (programs) are considered as the foundations for developing program objectives. Recommondations for writing program objectives complete the discussion.

SYSTEM GOALS

Recreation and leisure-service systems provide the leadership and the areas and facilities that enable people to engage in recreation behavior. The provision of service is based upon perceived need for recreation and a system's goals, which are related to needs. Goals establish the general purpose of an organization and provide the general guidelines for program planning. The needs-assessment process provides the programmer with an indiciation of the types of activities that will satisfy recreation needs. In planning recreation programs, the programmer attempts to go beyond providing activities to providing individuals with opportunities that give their lives greater meaning. The recreation program ideally affords the individual an opportunity for self-expression; discovery; personal development; expansion of interests and social horizons; achievement; recognition; and the experience of joy, pleasure, and excitement. Concurrently, the goals of recreation and leisure services, and the provisions of relevant and responsive opportunities, serve to enrich the quality of life in any community. A system's goals generally express a concern for the general welfare of its constituents and how its services contribute to their well-being.

The principles of recreation provide the programmer with the fundamentals for developing program objectives. The general principles provide for:

1. Recreation leadership.
2. Opportunities for individuals to engage in recreation.
3. Opportunities for personal development.
4. Maximum use of resources.

5. Use and conservation of natural areas for recreation purposes.
6. Continuous evaluation.
7. Contingencies by developing alternative program plans.
8. Program promotion.

The principles provide guidelines for planning and conducting recreation activities so that the programmer and the participant mutually attain their respective goals. Incorporating the principles of recreation into the program's objectives is a logical process that will improve the quality of a recreation program.

On the basis of professional judgment, the programmer uses his or her training and knowledge of human behavior to develop program objectives that integrate a system's goals and perceived recreation needs into a functional plan of action. The conceptual abilities that a professionally prepared recreation and leisure-service specialist brings to the program-planning process enables that specialist to infer that there are specific recreation needs. Inference of need is based upon empirical evidence and the philosophical, psychological, and sociological principles that provide the foundations of recreation and leisure services.

The needs-and resource-assessment process provides the programmer with information to make decisions related to the selection of appropriate activities and the resources with which to implement programs. All of the activity opportunities, services, and facilities that enable people to individually and collectively engage in recreation and leisure behaviors are considered to be the program. Murphy and Howard explain the concept of a program as "the complex of opportunities usually including a broad range of organized activities (sports, arts and crafts, music, drama, etc.) as well as a variety of physical resources (swimming pools, recreation centers, playgrounds, etc.) all of which seek to enrich the quality of community life."[1] A comprehensive program provided by an agency will normally afford activity opportunities in the functional program categories of creative, cultural, educational, outdoor, physical, service, and social. A review of current literature and program brochures reveals some fourteen different types of recreation activities. These are as follows:

Arts and crafts	Music
Dance	Outdoor recreation
Drama	Physical fitness
Educational	Social recreation
Games	Special events
Hobbies and clubs	Sports and athletics
Homemaking	Vehicular recreation

In each category there are several alternatives for the distribution and delivery of services and various levels of involvement to be accounted for in the development of program objectives.

PROGRAM OBJECTIVES

Program objectives are the actual written plan for organizing and conducting recreation activities. They define a program's purpose, identify the population group served, specify procedures for conducting activities, and provide the standards for evaluating results. Program objectives identify who, what, where, when, why, and how activities will be organized; the anticipated results; and their general purpose. Ideally, they should be developed with and for an agency's participants and for each activity or service sponsored by an agency. Participant involvement in the process of developing program objectives is accomplished by the systems approach through the needs-assessment process and the general nature of the system, which encourages input by citizen-involvement planning techniques. Program objectives define the intent of a program and establish the criteria for determining when specific goals have been achieved.

In a discussion of the merits of performance objectives, Edginton, Compton, and Hanson propose the following:[2]

How can a recreation and leisure professional know when an end has been reached if no goals or objectives have been identified to indicate what that end was to be? More specifically, purpose, goals, objectives, and performance objectives must be established for three reasons: (1) to indicate the final end towards which the professional wishes the program to go; (2) to indicate how the intended results or end will be reached; and (3) to serve as a control, indicating whether the projected end has been reached.

Program objectives are concise written statements of purpose or intent, which Meger suggests should be observable, and measureable, with some dimension of time.[3] He suggests that useful instructional objectives have at least three components:

1. A description of the learner's behavior, which will be evidence that desired learning has occurred.
2. A definition of the conditions under which the behavior will occur.
3. A statement of the criterion or standard that will be used to judge performance.[3]

In writing objectives for recreation programming, Meger's concepts are paraphrased and expanded upon to eliminate oversight in the planning and organization of activity opportunities.

Normally, program objectives will be written using action verbs to describe

1. The activity that will be provided.
2. Who will participate and who will lead, supervise, or conduct the activity.
3. When and where it will occur and how long it will last.
4. What the requirements for participation are.
5. The procedures for conducting the activity.
6. The procedures for determining program effectiveness (evaluation).

In writing program objectives, the programmer will identify the activity and the participants skill or ability level that the program is designated to accommodate. This phase will be dictated by the program format. Farrell and Lundgren identified five procedures for conducting program activities: organized competition, classes, organized groups, special events, and open facilities.[4] There is an additional method to be considered—outreach—which is extending an agency's services beyond the boundaries of its facilities into the places that people congregate. Program planning requires a programmer to develop, in advance, a conceptual picture of what is to be accomplished and then list all of the tasks or requirements for producing or conducting an activity. Specifying and recording on a flowchart, or program planning from the different tasks involved, enables the programmer to establish the program's objectives. Determining how a program will be offered— class, interest group, league, or special event—and when and where may require the programmer to establish a list of program priorities. The program format will determine the requirements for leadership, materials, equipment, and facilities that will best meet the needs of the participants and enable the programmer to specify the procedures for conducting an activity or program.

In writing program objectives that are observable, measurable, and have a time factor, the programmer may describe participant activity in instructional, behaviorial, or performance objective terms. Bloom's *Taxonomy of Educational Objectives* has been used to analyze recreation behavior to determine the major requirements to successfully engage in an activity.[5] Recreation activities involve aspects of a person's cognitive, affective, and psychomotor skills. In developing program objectives, the programmer will specify in advance the recreation need to be addressed, the activity to be provided, who will participate, when and where the activity will occur, its duration, and the criteria for its evaluation. In writing program objectives, the programmer may list the skills involved, or those to be developed or reviewed, or specific objectives he or she wants to accomplish by using an adaptation of Bloom's taxonomy. An example follows:

1. Cognitive skills involve one's knowledge and understanding and are classified as:
   a. Knowledge: knowing the rules.
   b. Comprehension: demonstrating the ability to follow directions.
   c. Application: demonstrated by correctly addressing a golf ball and correctly swinging a club.
   d. Analysis: the ability to recognize an opponent's strategy and counteract it.
   e. Synthesis: bringing together the component parts of a creative project.
   f. Evaluation: the ability to make value judgments.
2. Affective skills involve one's feelings, emotions, and values and are categorized as:
   a. Receiving: personal awareness of verbal and nonverbal messages.
   b. Responding: becoming involved in a recreation experience in terms of its physiological, social, or psychological benefits.
   c. Valuing: assigning a value to the recreation experience in terms of its physiological, social, or psychological benefits.
   d. Organizing: the development of a consistent value system.
   e. Characterization: a commitment to regular involvement in recreation activity.
3. Psychomotor skills, which include organic and physiological development, involve one's physical and neuromuscular skills and are classified as:
   a. Imitations: imitation of some observed act.
   b. Manipulation: performing a particular skill.
   c. Precision: accuracy in performing a skill.
   d. Articulation: coordination of a series of acts.
   e. Naturalization: the smooth and natural performance of a skill, or responding instinctively to a stimulus.

Identification of the skills involved in recreation activity enables the programmer to specify how various skills will be improved. Edginton and Hayes suggest that performance objectives based on the taxonomy of educational objectives can be used to account for the behavior that will result from an activity experience.[6] The programmer will project that an activity will result in a set of positive behaviors that contribute to the attainment of a system's goals.

When concise statements of anticipated program results are developed in advance to specify what will occur, when it will occur, when it will end, and how a program will be conducted, the criteria for evaluating a program are established.

WRITING PROGRAM OBJECTIVES

In writing program objectives, the programmer will develop concise descriptive statements related to what the participants will do, what the leader will do, how the agency will support the activity, and how the program will be evaluated. In defining participant behavior or activities, Edginton and Hayes suggested that the following four factors be included in writing performance objectives:

1. What must be known or done by the (participant) client?
2. How is the (participant) client to demonstrate a specific behavior?
3. What condition or circumstance may affect the acquisition and demonstration of a specific behavior?
4. What is the minimum level of acceptable achievement for the (participant) client's performance of a given behavior?[6]

These four factors of performance objectives were developed for the therapeutic recreation setting where behavioral change was emphasized. The programmer in a community setting should not develop statements that superimpose a set of values or expectations on participants that are beyond the ordinary participant's ability. He or she should advocate assertive discipline and use general terms to describe participant behavior when writing program objectives for the public at large.

The program objectives for a tennis class will specify the skill level, population served, time, dates, place, class content, methods of organization, and administrative policies and procedures. Program objectives for a beginner's tennis class include the following:

1. Identification of the population to be served and the number of participants accommodated per class.
2. A description of the skills to be taught by instructors. Beginning tennis classes involve teaching the grips, forehand and backhand strokes, serve, rules, and court etiquette.

3. Information pertaining to time, dates, place of instruction, and practice and playing time. The number of classes provided will also be specified.
4. Procedures for conducting the classes will be identified and the physical, social, and emotional benefits derived from playing tennis will be described.
5. Procedures for registering, dates, fees charged, and agency administrative policy and procedures are specified. The agency will specify what participants must provide (rackets, balls, and shoes, for example).

Following the outlined tennis class objectives, the programmer, instructor, and participants will have a general understanding of the who, what, where, and when of beginning tennis.

Program objectives are modified and used as behavioral and performance objectives to move a program closer to goal attainment. Behavioral and performance objectives are more precise statements that describe behavior and performance. Action verbs are used to construct concise descriptive statements of the behavior or action that will occur during and as a result of recreation experience. A beginner's swimming class serves as a model for illustrating how program, behavioral, and performance objectives are interrelated in planning, and how they are used.

1. The program objective is to *provide* swimming lessons to enable participants to become water-safe so that they can enjoy swimming, bathing, and aquatic sports.
2. The behavioral objectives serve to control the participants in and out of the water, before, during, and after swimming classes. In this case, behavioral objectives are the safety rules that govern all swimming-pool activities.
3. The performance objectives specify the action required to swim. Swimming skills are broken into specific actions, i.e., rhythmic breathing, the prone glide, back float, arm strokes, kicks, changing directions, front dive, and combining (synthesis of) skills which are required to propel oneself through the water. The skills are defined, described, demonstrated, practiced, and mastered in the process of learning and teaching swimming.

There are twenty skill competencies to be mastered prior to completing the American Red Cross beginner swimming test, and standards of performance are defined for each skill on a checklist. Checklists similar to swimming-skill sheets can be obtained or developed to observe and record other recreation behaviors or performances using standards as the criteria for evaluation.

Standards are specific units of measurement and are used in conjunction with program objectives to evaluate recreation programs. Standards for most recreation activities are based on average performance, routine behavior, rules and regulations, and experience. Procedures for evaluating recreation are inherent in each phase of the systems approach to program planning and the techniques for comprehensive evaluation will be discussed in the final phase, feedback and continuous evaluation. Standards are used to evaluate behavior and performance when developing program objectives.

Edginton and Hayes suggest that, for purposes of evaluation, program objectives should describe observable behavior.[6] How a participant is to change as a result of recreation experience (what a person will demonstrate or exhibit at the conclusion of a session or a program) should be specified. Refer to a list of illustrative verbs developed by Claus (see *Stating Behavioral Objectives for Classroom Instruction,* by Norman E. Gronland), which provides an example of action verbs used in writing program objectives. Six different recreation behaviors and illustrative verbs were used by Edginton and Hayes to describe the content of performance objectives. The following are examples abstracted from the list:

1.   Creative behaviors: change, design, rearrange, synthesize.
2.   Social behaviors: communicate, dance, discuss, interact.
3.   Music behaviors: clap, harmonize, play, sing, whistle.
4.   Physical behaviors: hit, pitch, catch, stretch, swing.
5.   Art behaviors: assemble, construct, form, paint, sketch.
6.   Drama behaviors: act, display, express, perform, show.

The programmer can use any action verb to describe the expected results of recreation experiences when writing program objectives.

To specify the minimum level of acceptable behavior or performance, three factors are used to determine proficiency—quantity, quality, and time or speed. Quantitative measurement reveals accuracy and precision, and provides nominal data. Qualitative measurement involves subjective speculation about the degrees of excellence and the final measurement establishes a time factor in seconds, minutes, hours, days, weeks, or number of trials.

All program objectives are subject to objective, subjective, qualitative, and quantitative evaluation. The criteria for evaluating a program are simultaneously developed when program objectives are developed.

SUMMARY

Program objectives are developed in the third phase of the systems approach to recreation programming. They integrate a system's purpose (goals), the principles of recreation, and recreation needs into a plan that uses resources to provide reponses and opportunities that define the expected results and procedures for organizing to achieve them.

The goals, principles, recreation needs, and concepts of programming provide the foundations for developing objectives. Normally program objectives will specify: (a) the activity, (b) the participants, (c) the setting, (d) the requirements for participating, (e) the procedures for conducting an activity, and (f) the criteria for evaluating program effectiveness. The programmer determines the program format in this planning phase.

The taxonomy of educational objectives provides a method of defining the behaviors involved in recreation activities. Using the taxonomies, a programmer can determine the cognitive, affective, and psychomotor aspects of an activity to determine how to plan to achieve the positive effects of recreation experiences. Concepts of instructional, behavioral, and performance objects were discussed to provide a broad perspective for writing program objectives. Several illustrative action verbs were listed as examples of the wording that can be used.

Program objectives enable a programmer to focus on achieving a system's goals and participant's needs while planning recreation activities. The development and use of program objectives enhances the effective and responsive planning of activity opportunities for people, individually and collectively.

ENDNOTES

1. Murphy, J. F., & Howard, D. R. (1977). *Delivery of community leisure services,* (p. 179). Philadelphia: Lea & Febiger.
2. Edginton, C. R., Compton, D. M., & Hanson, C. J. (1980). *Recreation and leisure programming,* (pp. 92-96). Philadelphia: Saunders College.
3. Meger, R. F. (1962). *Preparing instructional objectives,* Palo Alto, CA: Fearson Publishers.
4. Farrell, P., & Lundegren, H. M. (1983). *The process of recreation programming.* (2nd ed., pp. 38-44). New York: John Wiley and Sons.
5. Bloom, B. S. (1956). *Taxonomy of educational objectives: handbook I.* New York: David McKay Co., Inc.

6.   Edginton, C. R., & Hayes, G. A. (1973). Using performance objectives in the delivery of therapeutic recreation services. *Journal of Leisureability,* 20-26.

8

ACTIVITY ANALYSIS

The personal satisfaction inherent in planning, organizing, and conducting a recreation activity in which there is congruency between a system's goals and objectives and the participants' needs is one of the intangible rewards derived from a leadership position. The first three phases of the systems approach—defining its purpose, identifying recreation needs and resources, and writing program objectives—enables a programmer to arrange a variety of responsive activities. The decision to proceed with the production of a program is normally a matter of professional judgment. The fourth phase of the systems approach to recreation programming involves the activity and cost analysis, which refines the decision-making process. The activity and cost analysis are processes that deterrmine the feasibility of producing activities and assure the programmer that the activities planned will contribute to the attainment of a system's goals and will enrich the recreation experience.

The procedures initiated to analyze planned activities and their cost are discussed in this chapter. Activity analysis and cost-benefit analysis are two procedures that provide a basis for making rational decisions related to the production of recreation activities.

ACTIVITY ANALYSIS

Gunn and Peterson define "activity analysis as a process for breaking down and examining an activity to find inherent characteristics that contribute to program objectives."[1] The activities projected for the program complex are analyzed to identify the specific requirements for participating, their inherent behaviors, and those that they will produce.

The physical activity and psychomotor behavior inherent in most recreation activities are perhaps easiest to identify and analyze. They include, but are not limited to, gross and fine motor movements and coordination, speed, strength, endurance, and conditioning. The physical requirements for participating and the skills developed during participation can be analyzed. The cognitive, intellectual aspects of recreation activity are identified concurrently and analyzed. The ability to comprehend rules and regulations, follow directions, and use strategies are some of the cognitive aspects inherent in participation that can be analyzed to determine if an activity is compatible with the participants' abilities, readiness, and maturity levels. Information from the needs-assessment process, the programmer's understanding of human development, and the environmental conditions that influence participants will allow the programmer to modify or adapt an activity so that it will satisfy the special needs of the participants. The activity analysis enables the programmer to change an activity on occasion so that it is more suitable for meeting the needs of participants. The decision to participate in a recreation activity is a cognitive process and a programmer understanding human motivation can use the activity analysis to identify elements of an activity that can be used to stimulate interests and encourage participation.

Recreation experiences are characterized as positive, fun-filled, enjoyable, and socially rewarding endeavors; therefore, the affective aspects of recreation behavior should be considered in analyzing an activity. The process determines if there are opportunities for the individual to derive from the experience a sense of achievement, success,and social acceptance, and to realize his or her human potential. In any human endeavor where there are positive experiences, there are also negative possibilities. The process enables the programmer to identify the negative aspects inherent in any activity. Briefly, these negative aspects are fear, anxiety, anger, frustration, and the possibility of failure. Identifying possible negative aspects of any activity enables the programmer to plan to control activities. The program leader and the participants are encouraged to use the concepts of assertive discipline to control situations that produce negative behavior.

Most recreation activities evolve around and promote social interaction. The social aspects of recreation activity, according to Gunn and Peterson, are as follows:[2]

1. Facilitation of social interaction by proximity
2. Opportunities for interacting with the opposite sex
3. The verbal communication required
4. The number of participants required
5. The physical contact inherent in activities

Peterson stated that activity analysis provides the programmer with an understanding of the inherent qualities of an activity, the factors involved in participation, and the outcome possibilities. According to Peterson, activity analysis will provide for:[3]

1. A better comprehension of the expected outcomes of participation.
2. A better understanding of the activity itself, which provides directions for leadership, instruction and intervention techniques, or other considerations in providing recreation opportunities.
3. A greater understanding of the level of skills and the complexity of an activity, which can then be compared with the functional level of an individual or group to determine the appropriateness of an activity for inclusion in a program.
4. An understanding of the elements or components of the activity, which gives directions for the modification or adaptations of that activity for an individual or group of participants.
5. Information regarding the appropriateness of that activity in moving toward the stated objectives, when program, behavioral, instructional, or performance objectives are used.

The procedure used to analyze recreation activities was developed by Avedon, and consists of ten steps. The following elements of an activity are identified by the analysis:[4]

1. The purpose, aim, or goals of an activity.
2. The procedures, methods, courses of, and patterns of action or manipulation.
3. The rules governing action, procedures that fix principles of behavior; rules also require behavioral change (repetitions), reinforcement of instructional or procedural sequence.
4. Required number of participants—maximum, minimum.
5. Role of participants, whether active or passive, the different positions and functions required, and the strategies involved. In certain activities, all participants assume the same role; there are numerous roles in other activities and different roles involved in recreation activities.
6. The results or outcomes of involvement, the reward or payoff as a direct or indirect result of involvement; biophysical, psychological,

intellectual, emotional, such as winning, gaining status through achievement, accomplishment, or relief.

7. The abilities, knowledge, and/or skills required to participate. Identifying the cognitive, affective, and psychomotor aspects of an activity is essential to reduce the risk inherent in any activity and to establish rational prerequisites for participating.

8. The patterns of individual and social interaction involved in the activity are explained below.

9. The physical setting, area, or facility that best accommodates an activity.

10. The amount and type of supplies, equipment, and materials required to conduct an activity.

This procedure for systematically breaking down an activity can be used to analyze any functional type of recreation event—creative, cultural, educational, outdoor, physical, service, and social recreation activities. An example follows a discussion of the interactive processes.

In addition to the procedures used to analyze activities, Avedon identified and explained the patterns of interaction that are inherent in recreation behaviors. He states:[5]

> Within each of the organizational patterns, certain interactive processes are inherent or can be superimposed. The interactive process limits, influences, or regulates the behavior of a person engaged in the process. There are eight interactive processes identifiable at this time.

The patterns of interaction Avedon identified and used to analyze recreation and other human behavior are as follows:[6]

1. *Intra-individual.* Action taking place within the mind of a person or action involving the mind and a part of the body but requiring no contact with another person or external objective.

2. *Extra-individual.* Action directed by a person toward an object in the environment, requiring no contact with another person. This process in inherent in reading, walking, mostly solitary art or craft activity, viewing television alone, and so forth.

3. *Aggregate.* Action directed by a person toward an object in the environment while in the company of other persons who are also directing action toward objects in the environment. This process is inherent in motion picture viewing, watching a play, in a bingo game, in a craft shop, and so forth.

4. *Inter-individual.* Action of a competitive nature directed by one person toward another . . .it is inherent in chess, checkers and a variety of two-person games.

5. *Unilateral.* Action of a competitive nature among three or more persons, one of whom is the antagonist or "it."
6. *Multi-lateral.* Action of a competitive nature among three or more persons, with no one person an antagonist. This is typical of a card game.
7. *Intra-group.* Action of a cooperative nature by two or more persons intent upon reaching a mutual goal. Action requires positive verbal and nonverbal interaction. This is the process required in interview structure and in a variety of activities such as playing in a band, singing in a choir, acting in a play.
8. Inter-group. Action of a competitive nature between two or more introgroups. This is the process inherent in team games such as basketball or bridge.

Programmers analyzing recreation activities will discover the requirements for conducting an activity and the results to be expected. The general requirements for promoting and conducting activities are leadership; areas and facilities, and supplies, equipment, and materials. Figure 8.1 illustrates a partial analysis of three activities—basketball, drawing, and social dancing.

	ACTIVITY		
Element	**Basketball**	**Drawing**	**Social Dancing**
Purpose	Score	Create	Interact
Procedure	Shooting	Manipulation	Movement
Rules	2 halves		Rhythm
No. of participants	5 per team	1 or more	Unlimited
Roles	Active	Active	Active
Reward	Physical	Accomplishment	Social
Abilities	Psychomotor	Cognitive	Affective
Interactive	Intergroup	Extra-Ind.	Inter-Ind.
Place	Gymnasium	Anywhere	Large hall
Equipment	Ball & baskets	Paper & pencil	Stereo

FIGURE 8.1   *Partial analysis of three activities.*

The activity analysis provides the programmer with an understanding of how an activity will satisfy the needs of a participant(s), the system's goals, and the program's objectives. In addition to revealing the requirements for conducting an activity, activity analysis enables the programmer to project a program's life cycle. Howard and Crompton found that programs go through four stages of development: introduction, take off, maturation, and saturation.[7] In a fifth stage a program will be extended, there will be a decline, it will become petrified, or it will become extinct. Through analysis of an activity, a programmer can plan to extend a program's life cycle. For example, in a southern California community where an extensive learn-to-play tennis program was provided by the parks and recreation department for beginners, the activity analysis revealed that, on completion of lessons, intermediate and advanced players and other players had no organized program in which they could participate. Continued interest in tennis was confirmed by the needs assessment and the programmer initiated a program for intermediate and advanced players to provide them with information about making court reservations, local tournaments, and clubs. This enabled the players to continue playing without a direct dependency on the department's program.

The potential opportunities for participants to engage in and to develop meaningful social relations is also assessed by the activity analysis. There is speculation that many organized recreation programs provide opportunities for people of all ages to meet people with similar interests and to become socially active in community life. Instructor and participant evaluations of user-fee adult classes have indicated that the opportunity for social involvement is just as important as the skill or knowledge acquired during a class.

Activity-analysis procedures enable a programmer to determine the inherent values associated with an activity, and its appropriateness, and enables him or her to proceed with an investigation of the requirements for producing it. Procedures for determining the cost and benefit of an activity, which are a prerequisite for making an operational decision, are discussed in the next section.

COST-BENEFIT ANALYSIS

The activity analysis provides the programmer with information to select activities that fulfill the requirements of the system's goals and program objectives, plus the needs of the participants. The decision to implement an activity is dependent upon whether it is administratively feasible to conduct it. To determine feasibility, the programmer will analyze the cost inherent in producing an activity in relation to projected benefits. Benefits are projected outcomes specified by program objectives and confirmed by the activity analysis. Cost equals the total expenditures in dollar amounts for personnel services, supplies, equipment, and materials—the total requirements for conducting an activity for a given period.

Cost-benefit analysis is a method of measuring user satisfaction, and consists of the projected benefits and program cost, and the effectiveness with which all resources are used. Meserow, Pompel, and Riech proposed that "benefits are measured in participant hours."[8] Perceived benefits may be projected by using a Nash-Shannon Pyramid of Leisure. Figure 8.2, the Nash-Shannon pyramid, is used for inferring values about the quality of an activity and assigning it a numerical weight. According to Shannon, start "with activities involving the highest form of creativity, assign a weight factor of eight. Lower the scale on a graduated basis to the activities in which an individual will participate to escape from monotony and boredom."[9] In assigning a value to an activity, Shannon used this formula: popularity percent × quality weight = index value. The popularity of an activity is multiplied by the assigned quality weight.

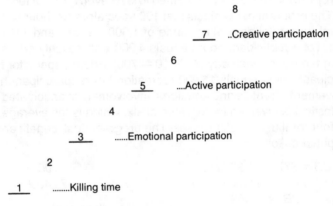

FIGURE 8.2   *The Nash-Shannon pyramid.*

According to Shannon:[9]

1. Popularity percent: Determine the popularity percent by comparing the number of participants in the activity to the total number of participants in the entire recreation program. This ratio will give the popularity percentage.
2. Quality weight factor. The numerical figure arrived at by comparing the activity to the quality spectrum.
3. Index value. The index value is the priority indicated for each activity.

When planning activities, the popularity percent is projected on program records or anticipated participation.

Cost benefit is determined by dividing the total cost by participant hours using the following formula.

$$CB = Program\ Cost/PC \qquad CB$$
$$Participant\ Hours/PH \qquad PH$$

The Shannon index value is then added to this formula by multiplying participant hours by the index value, creating a new formula.

$$CB = Program\ Cost \qquad = CB$$
$$Participant\ Hours \times Index\ Value \qquad (PH \times IV)$$

The following example is provided to illustrate the process; it represents a hypothetical situation.

A community arts festival is planned for a total cost of $700 with seventy artists participating by demonstrating, performing, or exhibiting their skills or works. The festival is planned to last seven days, for ten hours per day. The programmer projects that 100 spectators per hour will visit the festival for a total daily attendance of 1,000 per day and 7,000 for the week. Total participant hours equals 4,900 with seventy artists participating ten hours each day ($70 \times 10 = 700$). Adding spectator hours to participant hours equals 11,900 recreation hours (participant hours) of involvement. Creative and emotional involvement is anticipated and the arts festival is given an index value of six, which is the average of eight and four for illustrative purposes. The program cost-benefit analysis is computed as follows:

$$CB = PC \quad = \quad \$700.00 \qquad\qquad 700$$
$$PH \times IV \qquad (11,900 \times 6) \qquad\qquad 71,400$$
$$CB \ = \ 0.009$$

The example illustrates that the arts festival would cost less than one cent per participant hour and that the fiscal resources were effectively used to provide a quality experience. In cost-benefit analysis, the lower the numerical value, the greater the benefit.

The procedures involved in the cost-benefit analysis require the programmer to determine all the costs involved in the development of a program or activity. This includes the administrative overhead, expenses incurred for leadership, planning time, secretarial time, layout and reproduction cost, and telephone calls. Also included are personnel expenses for the total hours involved in preparing for an activity and conducting it, including personnel benefits, routine maintenance and operational expenses for supplies, equipment, utilities (heat, water, electricity), insurance, and other program costs, which are prorated on the basis of time. The prorated cost based on personnel time and the actual cost of supplies are computed to obtain the program cost figure.

Activity analysis provides the basis for decision making—determining the administrative feasibility of promoting an activity. An activity is administratively feasible to promote when the predictable results in terms of needs satisfaction are compatible with the system's goals and program objectives, there are resources to produce it, and there are no exceptional risks involved. In developing a comprehensive recreation program, every conceivable activity should be analyzed, and the programmer proceeds to produce those that satisfy the criteria established by the system. These criteria usually include:

1. Adequate opportunities for human growth and development, and the satisfaction of personal needs for physical, social, cultural, intellectual, and other experiences.
2. Making a contribution toward improving the quality of life.
3. Adequate financial resources to support the program and proper procedures to account for all funds received and expended.
4. A rational plan for area and facility maintenance.
5. Feasible activity schedules, including leadership assignments and other program requirements.

When the above requirements are satisfied, the programmer is ready to proceed with the operational planning phase of the systems approach to recreation programming.

SUMMARY

Activity and cost-benefit analysis, the two procedures completed in the fourth phase of the systems approach to recreation programming, provide a basis for selecting the activities to be included in the program. The activity analysis procedure has primarily been used for prescriptive programming for therapeutic recreation purposes. The effectiveness of this procedure in designing therapeutic programs suggests that all programmers should analyze activities to determine the effect that an activity will have on participants.

The cost-benefit analysis procedure enables the programmer to determine the financial feasibility of producing an activity or program. The process accounts for the anticipated cost of producing an activity while satisfying participants' needs, system's goals, and program objectives. It provides also for calculating user fees when an activity must be offered as a self-sustaining program.

Activities found to be financially feasible as well as compatible with the systems purpose are organized in the next phase of the systems approach.

ENDNOTES

1. Gunn, S. L. & Peterson, C. A. (1984). *Therapeutic recreation program design*, (p. 180). Englewood Cliffs, NJ: Prentice Hall, Inc.
2. Gunn & Peterson, p. 169.
3. Peterson, C. A. (September 1974). *Activity analysis and prescriptive programming: State of the art.* Paper presented at the National Recreation and Park Association Research Needs Conference, Columbia, MO.
4. Avedon, E. M. (1974). *Therapeutic recreation service,* (p. 174). Englewood Cliffs, NJ: Prentice-Hall Inc.
5. Avedon, p. 162.
6. Avedon, p. 162-172.
7. Howard, D. R. & Crompton, J. L. (1980). *Financing, managing and marketing recreation and park resources,* (p. 378). Dubuque, IA: W. C. Brown Company.
8. Meserow, L. H., Pompel, D. T. & Riech, C. M. (February 1975). Benefit-cost evaluation. *Parks and Recreation, 10.* (2), 29, 40-41.
9. Shannon, A. (September 1975). A systems approach to recreation planning. *Parks and Recreation, (10).* 9, 32.

OPERATIONAL PLANNING

The fifth of the system's seven program-planning phases is operational planning. It is the process of organizing the resources that are required to produce activity opportunities for people. It is a continuation of the first four phases in which the system's purpose was defined, needs and resources were identified, program objectives were developed, and activities were analyzed. The programmer uses goals and needs to identify the activities that are responsive to the needs in the first two phases. In the third phase, program objectives are developed by incorporating needs, goals, and principles into statements of specific program purpose. The activities that will satisfy people's needs are identified in this phase. Activity analysis, the fourth phase of the process, enables the programmer to select the activities that are feasible to conduct and will concurrently satisfy recreation needs, program objectives, and the system's goals.

The first four phases of the system's approach to program planning provides the information the programmer uses to:

1. Identify activities that will satisfy recreation needs.
2. Organize, coordinate, and produce all the system's recreation programs.
3. Implement new activities and revise and improve the quality of existing programs.
4. Eliminate from the program those activities that are no longer feasible to conduct.

116

In the fifth phase, the programmer can use either the program evaluation review technique (PERT), the flowchart method (FCM), or any other program-planning method that will eliminate oversight in planning to organize the resources necessary to produce activities. The PERT chart, illustrated in figure 9.1, consists of a twenty-week planning phase.

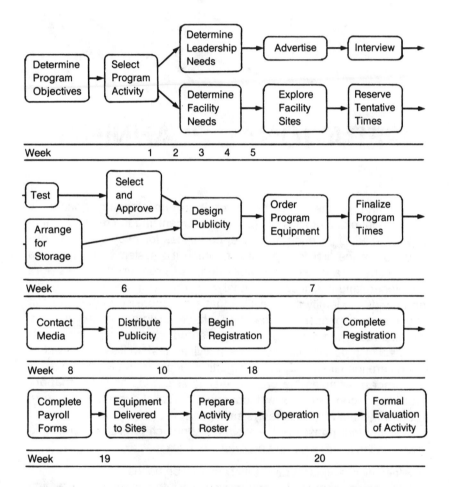

FIGURE 9.1 *Program evaluation review technique with critical path method.*

The PERT form with critical dates for accomplishing the various tasks was adopted from Farrell and Lundegren for developing a Hershey's National Youth Track and Field Meet for the City of Redondo Beach,

California, in 1983.[1] Benest, Foley, and Welton suggest using a format for planning, developing, and evaluating programs that consists of twelve vertical columns.[2] The columns are listed in the order in which they appear across the top of two eight-by-eleven-inch sheets of paper. The column headings are as follows:

1. Community problem
2. Indicator of need
3. Target population
4. Community, staff, and other input required
5. Program goals
6. Work activities
7. Timeline for work activities
8. Verifiable or measureable evaluation criteria
9. Documentation/Means of measurement
10. Resources required
11. Possible constraints
12. Results of evaluation[3]

Van Dinter developed an outline form for program planning purposes that consists of ten major sections. They are the following:

1. Objectives
2. Survey
3. Leadership
4. Facilities
5. Equipment
6. Schedule
7. Cost/budget
8. Promotion
9. Operations
10. Evaluation[4]

Murphy and Howard advocate using the flowchart method; a summer playground programs development is illustrated by figure 9.2.[5] The program evaluation review technique, flowchart method, the format for planning, and the outline are tools for accounting for all the variables that must be considered in program planning. The systems approach to program planning is a flexible method that will accept and use either of the methods outlined.

There are ten tasks to be accomplished in the operational planning phase to organize the resources necessary to produce recreation opportunities for people. The system uses human, fiscal, and physical resources to produce and support its programming effort.

HUMAN RESOURCES-PERSONNEL

First and foremost, the system is operated and controlled by the people who ultimately make the operational decisions. One professional programmer can generally plan a program; however, to accommodate all participants additional full-time, part-time, and voluntary leadership personnel are required to conduct or supervise the planned activities or facility use. The programmer must determine the exact leadership

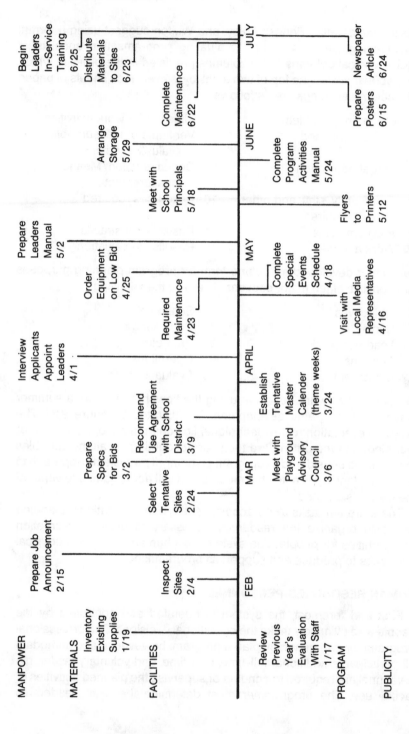

FIGURE 9.2 *Flow chart method, summer playground program.*

requirements for conducting the activities planned. Professional and/or paraprofessional personnel, recreation attendants, and aids or volunteers may be recruited for or assigned to various program responsibilities. Whether a programmer employs full- for part-time paid staff or uses volunteers in program leadership positions, the number to be used is dependent upon the intent and duration of the activity.

A programmer can recruit a staff and provide an intensive in-service training program for a playground program. On the other hand, depending upon the scope of an adult sports program, one paraprofessional part-time program supervisor can adequately work with a number of paid part-time officials and scorekeepers to run any competitive sports league. The teams will provide their own coaches and managers. From among the players, coaches, managers, and officials, the supervisor can organize the committees that will govern and administer the program within the system's policies. When a youth sports or instructional program is offered, the programmer may employ a number of part-time personnel to conduct activities at various sites. When offering classes, clinics, and workshop-type programs that are normally self-sustaining, the programmer must identify the instructors and supervisors to conduct ballet, gymnastics, ceramics, photography, piano, and other activities.

During the needs-assessment process, the programmer should attempt to identify individuals in the community who have the knowledge and skills to contribute to the program as a paid or volunteer leader. The system's personnel section can be used to provide the necessary personnel for part-time, seasonal, and full-time program positions, and must be operated in a manner that conforms to existing legislation. There are a number of legal considerations to be considered when employing personnel, especially the Civil Rights Act of 1964, the Vocational Rehabilitation Act, Vietnam Era Veterans Readjustment Act of 1974, the Age Discrimination in Employment Act of 1967, the Equal Pay, Affirmative Action, Equal Employment Opportunity Act, and others.

Whether one is recruiting volunteers or paid staff, it is advisable to advertise in the local newspaper to inform the public at large of the job opportunities. A personnel file system should be initiated for full-, part-time, and volunteer staff members, and an application retained for all personnel. The personnel management process involves:

1. Completing an application.
2. Reviewing or screening to determine which applicants are most or best qualified.
3. Interviewing qualified applicants, checking their references, and testing, if applicable.

4. Completing the selection process.
5. Thanking and informing individual applicants who cannot be used at present, as a matter of courtesy and good public relations.
6. Scheduling and completing staff in-service training and orientation.
7. Giving assignments to individuals and preparing for the participants.

Concerns such as wages or salaries, pay periods, work records or timekeeping procedures, and paydays should be covered during the general orientation or during a site orientation. Procedures for emergencies, personal sickness, personal holidays, and personal benefits (if applicable) should be discussed with each employee. Incentive programs for volunteers should also be outlined. In working with part-time and seasonal employees, it is essential to impress them with the fact that without their presence there will be no program and that recreation leadership is a very responsible position.

Programmers must develop a financial plan for securing all the resources required to conduct a program and control expenditures so that the allocated budget for the program is not exceeded. Personnel management, budgeting, and facility planning and development are subjects addressed in other professional preparation courses. In programming, the individual is concerned with using resources to serve the best interests of people and the system.

FACILITIES

The needs-assessment and resource-identification process provides the programmer with information about existing recreation areas and facilities. In the operational planning phase, the programmer will do the following:

1. Inspect and determine which of the areas and facilities will best accommodate the planned activities.
2. Select the facility that is most accessible to the participants. Arrange for its use by scheduling use of the system's controlled facilities or contracting for the use of other facilities.
3. Determine the maintenance requirements, schedule all routine maintenance to eliminate interference with program activities, and set a date for completion of facility preparation or daily setup by a specified time. If a room is to be used for more than one type of activity, plan for the take down and setup for each type of activity.
4. Inspect all facilities, areas, and equipment to ensure participant safety.
5. Inspect all utilities to ensure that they are in proper working order.

6. Specify procedures for securing a facility after its use, such as locking doors, turning off lights, and securing offices and office equipment.

SUPPLIES, EQUIPMENT, AND MATERIALS

The programmer should make an extensive list of equipment required, including balls, bats, and bases. A basic minimal softball program can be conducted with a softball, bat, bases, and an open field. The list is expanded to include such items as score books, schedules, league-standing posters, chalk for marking the field, supply items for the maintenance of rest rooms, trash bags for cans, extra balls, and bases when the programmer plans for a league to play two or three games on the same diamond daily. It is essential that supplies be planned to the nearest paint brush, box of construction paper, or paper clip. The programmer must inventory program supplies, equipment, and materials and determine the quantities needed, develop specifications for competitive bidding, select the best-quality item, purchase it from the best bid, inventory on receipt of the order, and store or distribute to program sites. If storage is necessary, he or she should arrange for the safekeeping of the item until it is needed and then distribute it to program sites, also developing a procedure for controlling the use of supplies and materials to prevent loss and theft.

SCHEDULING

Russell said, "Planning has worth if it leads to implementation."[6] Implementation depends upon scheduling, which involves determining the program format and the length, duration, day(s) of the week, and time of day an activity will be offered. Programs can be planned as classes, clubs or interest groups, competitive events, special events, outreach, and open facility. There are two principles involved in scheduling: (1) provide activity opportunities at times and places people can participate and (2) the schedule and program format should be compatible.

1. Classes, clinics, and workshops are generally scheduled for eight to ten weeks in the morning, afternoon, early evening, and evenings, Monday through Saturdays.
2. Special-interest groups and clubs normally require the use of meeting and activity places by time of day and day of the week or month, and they should be permitted to use a facility at the time requested.

3. Competitive activities, leagues and tournaments, and contests are scheduled as follows:

   a. Single-elimination tournaments, often with consolation tournaments for first-round losers. Single-elimination tournaments are arranged in bracket form and are the quickest method of determining a winner. The number of games to be played can be determined by subtracting one from the total number of entries. For example, with sixteen entries, fifteen games will be played. In determining the number of rounds required, the total should be the same number as the power to which two must be raised to equal the number of entries. For example, with eight contestants, two must be raised to the third power, indicating there will be three rounds. In the case in which there are only thirteen contestants, (see Figure 9.3), this total must be raised to sixteen, the next highest power of two. Thus, because 16 = 2, there will be four rounds. To calculate the number of games to be played in round one, subtract the number of byes from the number of teams or entries and divide by two (13 - 3 = 10 divided by 2 = 5 games). Byes are placed in the brackets as illustrated.

   b. Double-elimination tournaments take a longer period of time to complete, because each team or contestant must be defeated twice to be eliminated. The number of games to be played in a double-elimination tournament is determined by subtracting one from the number of entries and multiplying by two. Add one to this total for a possible championship playoff.

   c. Challenge-type tournaments, ladder, and pyramid can be used to sustain interest for long periods of time. They are normally used to stimulate interest of individuals involved in individual sports. One or more facilities may be required to sustain continuous activity.

   d. Round-robin tournaments require a longer period of time to complete and provide an opportunity for each contestant or team to play every other contestant or team. To determine the total number of games to be played, there are two formulas. The first is $N(N-1)/2$ with N representing the number of entries. In the second formula, record the number of entries 6, 5, 4, 3, 2, 1 and cancel the highest number, adding the remaining figures (5 + 4 + 3 + 2 + 1 = 15 games to be played). There are many different types of round-robin tournaments. One of the most common methods is to arrange the teams in two vertical columns, as follows:

1-4	5-1	1-6	3-1	1-2
2-5	4-6	5-3	6-2	3-4
3-6	2-3	4-2	5-4	6-5

The home team is listed on the left and times, courts, or fields of play are assigned. There are several variations for scheduling round-robin tournaments; these are often provided by major sporting goods stores.

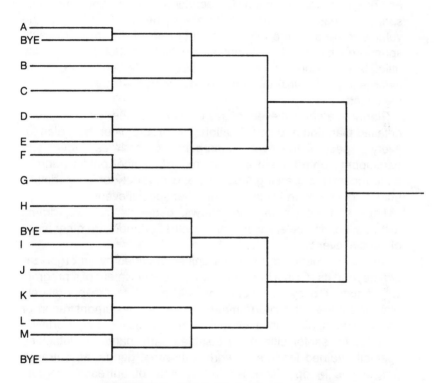

FIGURE 9.3 *Single-elimination tournament.*

4. Special events can be organized around any type of activity and are usually held to initiate or end a program. It is also the format used to conduct one-time annual events such as art festivals, tournaments, track and field meets, or other special performances. Normally, large numbers of spectators and participants are involved. Russell said, "One planning fact stands out when preparing the special event format, it is big. Bigness is what makes the event special."[7]

The Hershey's National Youth Track and Field Meet conducted by the Recreation and Parks Department in Redondo Beach, California, for example, involves 15 percent of the city's school-age children. The city's Youth Sports Associations (football, basketball, baseball, and soccer), the Boy and Girl Scouts, a marching group, and the schools all play a part in this meet. Teams representing the above organizations and volunteers from the sports associations, and civic and service organizations are involved as meet officials, emergency medical personnel, security personnel, and other personnel necessary to conduct the all-day affair. The efforts of the volunteers enable the city to conduct one of the largest events sponsored by the department at the high school stadium. City officials and former Olympians have also volunteered to present the awards to the contestants who finish among the top six in each of the events.

Planning a special event of this type or any other event requires detailed planning and coordination. The programmer must plan for every aspect of the event—emergency procedures, crowd and participant control, meet officials, recordkeeping, public address announcements, parking, security, and a variety of other details unique to a track and field meet or other special event.

Trips and excursions, pet shows, pageants, recitals, drama festivals, holiday celebrations, and award banquets are other types of special events.

5. Outreach is extending the opportunities provided by an organization beyond its normal boundaries. The specific intent of a program will dictate the special concerns addressed in the operational planning phase. If a programmer is planning a demonstration or conducting a class in a shopping mall, initiating transportation services for senior citizens or disabled participants, or detaching specially trained leaders to work with street gangs, an outreach program is in operation. Again, the type of outreach program planned will dictate the operational planning procedures.

6. Open facilities occur generally any time a recreation place is open for business and there are opportunities for people to drop in and participate or use areas, equipment, and facilities that are not being used for formal activities. Game rooms, swimming pools, playgrounds, tennis courts, and often golf courses provide participants with an opportunity to drop in and participate. For example, when tennis courts are not scheduled for use for instruction, league play, or tournament competition, an open facility exists that can be used by a participant for an hour or so. There are no set times for people

to be involved in activity when open facilities are provided. Policies should be established to govern the operations of facilities and restrict their use after 9, 10, or 11 P.M.

When scheduling the use of a facility, the programmer should make provisions that will enable people to engage in a variety of self-directed activities. The programmer should plan to accommodate as many participants as possible.

Playground programs are an important aspect of most recreation and leisure-service systems offerings. Normally, they are provided during the daylight hours during vacation periods. In addition to the traditional daylong program format in Kettering, Ohio, a "Play go' Round" program was initiated in 1982. According to Barnett, the program consisted of seven weeks during which five playground sites would be staffed with leaders in the morning; the leaders would "go-'round" to five other sites in the afternoon for four hours.[8] In Denton, Texas, the Parks and Recreation Department operates the summer playground program from 8:00 A.M. to noon Monday through Friday, and from 6:00 to 9:00 P.M. Monday through Thursday. In addition to these hours, the participants from each playground site go swimming one afternoon a week from 2:00 to 4:00 P.M. The split-session schedule is advantageous for several reasons. First, it allows for operating in the cooler parts of the day and second, evening hours allow for family participation.[9] In scheduling, a programmer should attempt to involve as many participants as possible while using resources responsibly.

PROMOTIONS

Procedures for promoting the program are planned in concert with the development of activity plans. Promotion involves developing an effective means of communicating with a system's constituents. It is essential that people be informed of and invited to participate in the planned activities. Normal procedures for promotion of a program include

1. Meeting with or visiting with representatives of the local media.
2. Preparing flyers, posters, newsletters, newspaper articles, and radio and television announcements.
3. Speaking to organized or assembled groups, such as the Parent Teachers Association, or civic and services organization meetings.
4. Word of mouth, the person-to-person approach by which people tell others about recreation opportunities.

The systems approach to program planning treats promotion and implementation as an independent planning phase. Procedures for promoting and implementing programs are outlined in chapter 10.

REGISTRATION

Program registration is the second of three implementation phases: Promotion is the first and beginning the program the third. Registration provides a means of accounting for the participants who will be involved in a program. If the class format is used, a minimum and maximum class size must be determined and registration will confirm whether a class will be conducted or not. Registration identifies participants by name, address, telephone number, age, and sex, and provides emergency data. It provides a method of organizing class rosters and collecting user fees. It also is a procedure for promoting other activities sponsored by an agency. The programmer determines the participant information that is needed, establishes a procedure, and determines the dates and places to collect it.

EMERGENCY AND RISK-MANAGEMENT PLANS

Risk is involved in all recreation activities and accidents do occur during recreation participation. Emergency and risk-management plans attempt to anticipate and prepare for any situation that may develop prior to, during, and after a recreation event. Lloyd said, "State laws vary on emergency care, but in general, facility operators can be held liable if they fail to provide reasonable response to life-threatening situations."[10] Programmers have a duty to protect participants from foreseeable dangers and to provide for the rapid response to emergency situations when emergency medical care is needed. Providing first aid and establishing procedures to handle serious emergencies is an essential aspect of program planning. Written guidelines should be developed to cover all possible emergencies.

There has been a dramatic increase in risk activities—hang gliding, parachuting, rock climbing, river rafting, scuba diving, skiing, and so forth—and plans must be prepared to provide for situations in which an emergency may occur. In risk programming, programmers may require participants to have medical examinations prior to participating and may require that participants take part in conditioning programs. Niepoth identified seven staff activities that serve to minimize the accident potential and avoid risks. They are as follows:

1. Identify possible hazardous areas and conditions.
2. Educate participants and staff for safe use.

3. Regulate or control use, when it is appropriate to do so.
4. Keep safety considerations in mind when planning facilities.
5. Implement appropriate maintenance practices.
6. Establish accident procedures.
7. Know your responsibilities.[11]

Activity analysis provides the programmer with a method of identifying possible hazards inherent in activities and developing procedures for reducing risks.

CONTINGENCY PLANS

Programmers must anticipate the unexpected when planning activities, and concurrently plan alternative activities that can be substituted when the primary program cannot be conducted. This is the process of planning rain dates for outdoor activities and arranging for alternative facilities to conduct planned and alternative activities.

IMPLEMENTATION AND DELIVERY

The process of providing relevant and responsive recreation opportunities for people, individually and collectively, involves knowing their needs, knowing when and where they can participate, and scheduling activities. When the operational planning phase is completed, the programmer initiates the promotional phase, conducts the registration phase, and initiates the activity.

EVALUATION

The process of defining a system's purpose and developing program objectives provides the criteria for measuring how successfully an activity or program has been planned and conducted. Procedures for evaluating recreation programs will be discussed in chapter 11.

Operational planning involves determining what must be done to implement a program and listing all the requirements for conducting it on a worksheet with a time line for completing each task. The time line or critical path involved will vary in length in relation to the activity being planned. Activities that require or are contingent upon special leadership, areas, facilities, supplies, materials, or equipment may require more time to organize than others. Another activity can be initiated with a minimum of delay when the resources are available. It is wise to allow extra time when a planned program's implementation is dependent upon the cooperation of another agency.

The systems approach to program planning encourages continuous review and examination of the system's goals, people's needs, and resources in the process or organizing activities. The review process may result in a decision to implement plans, delay implementation, or discontinue the planning process and start over so that a more responsive program can be offered. Each of the system's subsystems are involved in the decision-making process that occurs at the completion of the operational planning phase.

PROGRAM AUTHORIZATION

A system's chief administrator or manager is ultimately responsible for the output of recreation activities, programs, service, and the operation of facilities, and is directly involved in the final decision to implement a program. The final decision, unless a program is mandated by a board of directors or city council, is based upon a review of the completed plans. Completed program plans should include the following:

1. Planned provisions for conducting activity opportunities that will contribute to human growth and development by satisfying the participants' physical, social, creative, cultural, intellectual, and spiritual needs and interests.
2. The provision of programs and services that will contribute toward improving the quality of life in a community.
3. The identification of adequate interests and financial support to sustain activities for a specified period.
4. Provisions for accounting for all income and expenditures associated with producing an activity.
5. An adequate plan to maintain the recreation areas and facilities that will be used.
6. Provision for cancelling a self-sustaining program in which there is limited interest, which is a fact of business.

Operational plans that are usually approved represent the systematic development of recreation opportunities for people individually, who as participants normally engage in group activities.

SUMMARY

Operational planning is the process of determining what has to be done to provide an activity, and it involves organizing the appropriate resources to conduct activities. The programmer has the option of using any one of the methods to complete the operational planning phase.

The program evaluation review technique (PERT), flowchart method, the format, and the outline approaches provide a procedure for accounting for all the variables involved in planning. The ten planning tasks discussed provide the systems programmer with a method of charting in advance and accounting for the timely completion of all tasks. The programmer accounts for the leadership, facilities, and supplies required to produce a program. The program schedule, promotional materials, registration procedures, risk management, and emergency plans and plans for other contingencies are completed prior to program implementation. Advanced planning for program evaluation completes the operational planning phase of the systems approach to recreation program planning.

The authority to initiate the program planning process is derived from a system's goals; the decision to implement plans rests with a system's manager or policy-making board. It is essential that the operational plans for conducting any program be as complete and comprehensive as possible, because operational plans represent how a program will be supported and conducted. The details presented for a program approval may range from a one-line statement of objectives to a detailed outline of how each specific item is to be accomplished and when it will be completed.

ENDNOTES

1. Farrell, P., & Lundegren, H. M. (1983). *The process of recreation programming* (2nd ed., p. 272). New York: John Wiley and Sons.
2. Benest, F., Foley, J., & Welton, G. (1984). *Organizing leisure and human services*, (p. 99). Dubuque, IA: Kendall Hunt.
3. Benest, Foley, & Welton, p. 100.
4. Van Dinter, N. R. (n.d.). *Recreation programming, steps to planning.* Mimograph outline. University of Northern Colorado, Greeley, Co.
5. Murphy, J. F., & Howard, D. R. (1977). *Delivery of community leisure services,* (pp. 199-203). Philadelphia: Lea & Febiger.
6. Russell, R. (1982). *Planning programs in recreation,* (p. 237). St. Louis: C. V. Mosby.
7. Russell, p. 205.
8. Barnett, G. (February 1982). *1982 play-go-round program report.* City of Kettering, Parks and Recreation Division, Kettering, Ohio.
9. Division of Recreation and Leisure Studies. (October 23, 1979). *Denton summer playscene, final report.* Denton, TX: North Texas State University.
10. Lloyd, C. (May 1984). Emergency medical responses is a facility responsibility. *Athletic Business, 8* (5), 34.
11. Neipoth, E. W. (1983). *Leisure leadership,* (pp. 264-266). Englewood Cliffs, NJ: Prentice Hall, Inc.

10

PROMOTION AND IMPLEMENTATION

Recreation program planning requires the programmer to invest a substantial amount of time and effort to organize the resources necessary to produce programs and activities. The time and effort invested in planning is fruitless if people do not use available facilities or participate in planned activities. The sixth phase of the systems approach to recreation programming involves the detailed planning of how a program is to be promoted, and its implementation. The promotional process consists of informing, inviting, persuading, and reminding people individually and collectively about their recreation and leisure opportunities. Program implementation is the process of starting the program. The systems approach to program planning forces the programmer to consider how a program will be promoted and implemented in the operational planning phase. Promotion and implementation are considered as a separate planning phase because they represent a systems output, rather than input or transformation of needs and resources into activity opportunities. Promotion also logically precedes program implementation. Promotion is the one single factor that contributes most to successful programming, because there are numerous human interests that compete for the individual's attention, time, and involvement in contemporary society.

PROGRAM PROMOTION

Howard and Crompton said that "promotion is basically communications which seeks to inform, persuade and remind members of a potential client group of an agency's program and services."[1] Program promotion relies on establishing communications between an agency and its constituents. Owen, Page, and Zimmerman have described communications as a circular process that consists of six phases: *(a)* formulating the message, *(b)* encoding, *(c)* transmitting the message, *(d)* receiving, *(e)* interpreting the message, and *(f)* feedback.[2] Feedback is a response to the message, usually a second message transmitted to the original source confirming that the message was received and understood or requesting further clarification. Communication theory reveals that there are distinct levels of communication that range from a distant, public level to a personal level. In the process of promoting a recreation program, the programmer is required to communicate with constituents from a public level or distance to individuals on a personal level, using verbal, printed, and audiovisual messages to inform, invite, and persuade people to engage in recreation activities.

In developing the promotional message, the programmer must remember that people respond best to personal messages addressed to them and that recreation involvement is generally voluntary. He or she must also recognize that there are various agencies competing for a person's leisure and recreation involvement. Therefore, the message formulated to inform and invite people to participate should be designed to appeal to the individuals for whom the program was planned. There are four types of communications available to promote a recreation program:

1. *Verbal.* This is the most effective method, because it allows for two-way communications—person-to-person, or person-to-group contact, and immediate feedback and clarification; and it provides a means of increasing the programmer's exposure to the general public.

2. *Written communications.* The printed media provide for personalized but indirect contact with the person addressed, and written communications involve a delay in the delivery of the message. Written messages, letters, flyers, brochures, signs, posters, and banners should be clear and concise announcements consisting of who, what, where, when, why, and, sometimes how. They should attract a potential participant's attention and provide specific information. With the exception of banners, they should answer all

the standard questions a potential participant may ask about a particular service, while arousing interest in that activity.

3. *Visual communications.* Essentially, this is a one-way method of transmitting information through the use of posters, signs, pictures, and artifacts. The use of visual stimuli has not been thoroughly researched; however, recreation facilities have an appeal of their own and many participants will seek to use them when they are open and their locations known.

4. *Multimedia communications.* The electronic media that enable the programmer to combine verbal, written, and visual symbols have proven to be quite effective. Color slides; movies; video tapes with audio sounds, voices, and music; and carefully designed printed messages can be used to present a program to a potential group of participants because each element of the presentation is designed to reinforce the basic message; for example, "Recreation is fun for you, it's fun for me, see you Tuesday evening at the park, 6:30 P.M."

Program promotion involves getting the potential participants' attention and informing and inviting them to participate in the planned activities. In promoting a program, timing is an essential factor to consider. Although effective messages can be developed to attract attention, inform, invite, and persuade people to participate in recreation, the right time to promote a program is a matter of speculation. Programs can be promoted too far in advance of implementation and sometimes too late to effectively involve participants. Seasonal and traditional activities provide a basis for programming and, therefore, a basis for program promotion. The programmer should be aware of conflicting interests that may affect the reception and interpretation of his or her message. Although seasonal activities (baseball, for example) have a traditional season and many participants anticipate the beginning of the season, there are other activities that must be more vigorously promoted to enlist participation. The ideal time to promote an activity is between four and six weeks prior to its implementation date. This allows for a gradual buildup of interest prior to program registration or implementation.

The promotional message or strategy planned must get the potential participant's attention. The message must be easily understood, related to the participant's needs and interests, account for conflicts of interests, and assure each and every potential participant that the program is for the individual.

The programmer should plan to use all available methods of promotion to inform people about the recreation and leisure opportunities provided by the service system. It is universally understood that recreation programs are planned to satisfy the needs and interests of the various participant groups served by a system. The promotional message and the media used to transmit it to a target group should be appropriate for communicating with that group. The message should be clear, concise, and informative, and it should invite each potential participant individually. A word of caution: No matter how clear or informative a message, there will always be some confusion; the programmer must plan for accommodating those people who do not receive and interpret the promotional message clearly. Generally, a telephone number is provided and this provides one method of clarifying a misinterpreted message.

PROMOTIONAL METHODS

There are four methods normally used by recreation and leisure-service organizations to promote programs, services, and facilities. According to Howard and Crompton, these are "personal contact, advertising, incentives, and publicity."[3]

The most effective and influential method of promoting recreation and leisure services is personal contact or personal selling. Personal contact is generally referred to as word-of-mouth informing or advertising. This method of program promotion is or can be used by all personnel at all levels within an organization and is especially effectively used by direct leadership personnel. It relies on personal contact with an agency's constituents and delivering the program message directly. It also eliminates most misunderstandings and allows for immediate feedback. Leaders or instructors have direct contact with regular participants and can inform them of planned programs. Generally, when participants are satisfied with their recreation experiences, they become advocates of the program and tell their friends about their experiences and coming events. This is, in effect, a word-of-mouth method of program promotion.

Networking is another method of personal selling by which a programmer can promote a program. The programmer establishes a personal contact with influential community leaders, teachers, clergymen, civic, and social leaders, who are told about the program. In turn, they tell their contacts about the program or use their influence and positions to encourage people to participate or support the recreation and leisure-service system. Personal selling involves direct contact and enables one person to convince or persuade others to engage in recreation activities. Tillman said that persuasion "is a combination of fact and emotions."[4] The fact is that recreation activity will occur and the emotions equal the appeal of most recreation activities.

Through the needs-assessment process, programmers gain a general understanding of a community and its people, their needs, interests, customs, traditions, and values. This information is used to plan programs and to formulate promotional messages. The programmer uses his or her knowledge of people's needs and wants and formulates interest-arousing promotional messages.

Advertising is another method used to promote recreation programs and services. It usually involves the use of the mass media to reach a broad audience. Advertising in newspapers or on radio or television is expensive and as effective a means of promoting a program as any indirect method of communication. Most public and voluntary agencies limit their paid advertisements to newspapers and the other printed media. Generally, an agency will contact a printer to produce annual reports, program brochures, and newsletters. A few agencies use direct mail services to send program literature to every resident address in their service area. Commercial recreation agencies have successfully used radio and television commercials to advertise their programs and services, adding the cost of advertising to membership and user fees.

Public and voluntary agencies generally rely on free publicity gained through a good public relations program. Public relations is a mangement effort to develop a positive agency image by providing quality programs, services, and facilities. Public relations involves establishing good relationships with the general public, and an agency's constituents, and getting free publicity as a result of the favorable image created by the programs and services offered. Newspaper editors and managers of radio and television stations, who believe that recreation and leisure services are beneficial and enrich the quality of life, will support a good program. Radio and television stations that promote recreation programs generally do so by using some of their public service announcement slots. This informs the general public about general or special programs. Public relations involves a continued effort to sustain a favorable public image, a helping image that enables people to engage in and enjoy recreation experiences.

Howard and Crompton suggest that recreation and leisure-service agencies can use incentives to promote activities.[3] Normally, incentives are considered as something of financial value. Commercial agencies and health and fitness clubs, for example, advertise a two-month membership for the price of one as an incentive to join. Public and voluntary agencies sometimes use certificates and reduced registration rates for some programs to entice people to participate. They have also offered reduced rates for families with two or more members participating in user-fee programs.

Recreation and leisure-service organizations can use personal selling, advertisements, public relations, and incentives as methods of informing and involving people in activities. The message used to inform people should be motivating and striking, and should reveal the difference that recreation can make in a person's life.

There is a trend developing in some communities where recreation and leisure-service organizations use quarterly brochures to promote programs. These brochures have become more colorful; they are indexed and provide all the information needed for a person to choose a recreation program—the who, what, where, and when. The specific information provided addresses the needs and wants of participant groups, program offerings for preschool children to senior citizens, and lists special events. Registration information is provided for completing registration in person or by mail. Three examples follow.

IMPLEMENTATION

Promotion precedes registration and implementation by informing, encouraging, and enlisting participation. Registration is a process of collecting personal information that is used to organize participants into manageable groups. It enables an agency to collect user fees and disseminate additional information. The registration process provides a method of maintaining accountability as people confirm that they are interested in the planned activities. Implementation is the actual delivery of services, the involvement of people in the planned activities.

There are over 400 recreation activities that can be organized as components of a system's comprehensive program. The promotion and implementation phase of the systems approach is completed by providing a continuum of recreation activities. (A list of recreation activities appears in the appendix.) The continuum begins with direct services and progresses through outreach to referral and enabling services.

1. Direct services involves an agency assuming the responsibility of organizing and conducting activities. Examples of direct services are:
   a. The cafeteria approach, in which the agency organizes and directs the activities and people choose those that they like and participate. Classes, clinics, workshops, leagues, tournaments, contests, and facilities are organized to provide instructional activities and opportunities for people to participate in selected

activities. Organized activities are provided on a continuous basis by the sponsoring organization.

TUMBLING   FEE: $20 for 8 weeks

Below are two categories for the tumbling program which is designed to increase children's strength and coordination.

Beginning Level: No previous experience in tumbling, movement or dance.

Intermediate Level: Completed beginning tumbling.

Beginning — straddle walks, bridges, leaps, hops, skips, forward roll, and elementary backroll.

Intermediate — forward straddle rolls, backward rolls, donkey kick, balancing.

12 Wed. (Beg.) 2:15-3 p.m.	Fulton Cafe, Room A Ages 4-5
13 Wed. (Beg) 3:15-4 p.m.	Fulton Cafe, Room A Ages 3-4
14 Wed. (Int) 4:15-5 p.m.	Fulton Cafe, Room A Ages 4-5

Instructor: Cathi Williams

PRESCHOOL BALLET   FEE: $20 for 8 weeks

Learn beginning ballet steps and positions. Develop grace, coordination, flexibility, self-expression and a simple dance. Class culminates in Parent Performance Day.

15 Mon. 2:30-3:15 p.m.	Dominguez Bldg. Ages 4-5
16 Wed. 3:30-4:15 p.m.	Tulita Cafeteria Ages 5-6

Instructor: Beth Newell

PRESCHOOL TAP/BALLET   FEE: $20 for 8 weeks

Your child will enjoy learning basic tap steps, basics of ballet and creative movement. Class culminates in Parent Performance Day.

17 Thurs. 4:15-5:15 p.m.	Dominguez Bldg. Ages 5-7

Instructor: Beth Newell

PRESCHOOL ICE SKATING   FEE: $26 for 6 weeks

NEW CLASS! Children learn basic ice skating skills with the internationally famous Ice Capades easy method. Fee includes skate rental, half-hour lesson, and optional practice time on the day of the lesson. Classes begin April 23.

18 Mon. 4-4:30 p.m. Lesson 2:30-4 p.m. or Practice 4:30-5 p.m.	Ice Capades Chalet 550 Deep Valley Drive Court Yard Mall Rolling Hills Estates Ages 3-5

TOY LOAN

Borrow toys, games and books at no charge. The toy library, located at 2310 Rockefeller Lane (on the north side of Perry Park), give children experience in checking out and returning various types of games and toys. Toy loan is staffed by volunteers and is open Tuesday and Thursday, 2-4:30 p.m., 374-5468.

CLASSES BEGIN WEEK OF APRIL 9, 1984 UNLESS OTHERWISE INDICATED.

YOUTH AND TEEN CLASSES

Ages 6 to 17 (Registration information on Page 7)

ART

DRAWING AND PAINTING   FEE: $19 for 8 weeks

Students develop their artistic talents and design sense using paper, pencil and watercolors.

19 Thurs. 4-5 p.m.	Tulita Cafe Ages 6-8
20 Thurs. 3-4 p.m.	Tulita Cafe Ages 9-12

Instructor: Mary Hauck

DANCE

JAZZ DANCE   FEE: $18 for 8 weeks

NEW CLASS! Come join this energizing after-school class in dance fitness. Class includes warm-up, toning exercises and simple dance routines.

21 Thurs. 4-5 p.m.	Fulton Cafe, Room A Ages 10-14

Instructor: Leslie Becker

MUSIC

GUITAR   FEE: $19 for 8 weeks

Learn basic chording, strumming, picking, and fundamentals using a variety of folk songs and popular music. Individualized help plus group instruction. Furnish your own guitar and music stand.

22 Wed. 5:15-6:15 p.m.	Fulton Cafe, Room B Ages 9-15

Instructor: Glenn Stiglic

YOUNG REDONDOANS!   FEE: $25 for 8 weeks

NEW CLASS! Perform upbeat, contemporary "Young Americans" type music in singing and dance. Class culminates in performance.

23 Thurs. 4-6 p.m.	Beryl Cafeteria Ages 9-13

Instructors: Dianne Curwick and Mike Walker

DRAMA

DRAMA PRODUCTION   FEE: $25 for 8 weeks

NEW CLASS! Perform a contemporary comedy-drama about self image. Exciting and fun!

24 Tues. 3:30-5:30 p.m.	Hillcrest Cafeteria Ages 10-14

Instructor: Tracy Evans

ACTING SKILLS FOR COMMERCIALS   FEE: $16 for 6 weeks

Learn introductory skills for acting in commercials: pantomime, script studies, concentration, developing scenes. Get comfortable performing in front of a camera.

25 Mon. 3-4 p.m.	Alta Vista Cafeteria Ages 6-9

Instructor: Rebecca Dutcher

Note. From Redondo Beach, California, Spring 1984, "Recreation Program and City Newsletter," p. 10.

Park Programs

Program Supervisors: Chad Brown, Genise Cummings
Call 830-7600, Ext. 225, for more information

Highlighting park programs will be activities designed especially for the entire family. The following classes are just a few of those offered at each park. For a complete schedule of classes, programs and excursions, contact the individual park at phone numbers listed below.

ANDERSON PARK

19101 S. Wilmington Avenue - (213) 639-0001
Center Director - Taavasa Mamea, "Jr."
Assistant Center Director - Valerie Davis

HOURS OF OPERATION

Monday-Friday . . . . 3:00 p.m. - 9:00 p.m.
Saturday . . . . 10:00 a.m. - 5:00 p.m.
Sunday . . . . 12:00 Noon - 5:00 p.m.

BIKE CLUB

The club will run every Wednesday and Saturday from 5:00 p.m. Activities will include Riding for Fun, Bike Moto Cross, and many other fun activities. All ages are welcome.

BOXING AND WEIGHTLIFTING

This Fall will be running every Tuesday and Thursday from 5:00 p.m.-7:30 p.m. Some of the activities are as follows: Lifting for Fitness, Aerobics, Boxing, and many other new activities. All ages are welcome.

ARTS AND CRAFTS

Arts and Crafts will be running every Monday and Wednesday from 4:00-5:00 p.m. Different varieties of Fall themes for crafts will be done this year.

SATURDAY BREAKFAST BOWLERS

Back by popular demand! This activity offers to the community a bowling league that is unique. For a nominal fee of $5.00 breakfast and 3 games and shoes every Saturday morning. Times for this activity will run from 10:00 a.m.-2:00 p.m. All ages welcome.

BOXING AND WEIGHLIFTING PROGRAM

This program is offered for anyone who is interested in conditioning their body and learning the skills of boxing. You have a choice of boxing or weightlifting or both. Contact park personnel for day and time.

YOUTH COUNSEL AFFAIRS SESSION

For those youth between the ages of 13 to 18 who would like to voice their opinion about their problems, likes and dislikes, along with discussions on events that are taking place in our society today. Guest speakers, excursions and films are all part of this teen activity. Classes will take place on a weekly basis.

DRAMA WORKSHOP

For those talented youth interested in performing in the annual drama production, classes will be scheduled to assist youth in the various aspects of the theatre.

WOODCRAFT

Experience the joy of making wood crafts. Participants will be encouraged to use their own imaginations to create unique wood crafts. Project materials and instruction will be provided.

TENNIS CLINIC

Come participate in this special program being offered to boys and girls ages 8-12. Learn the basic techniques of tennis. This class is for beginners only. Call Avalon Park for further information.

SPECIAL EVENTS

Annual Drama Production (date to be announced).
Annual Halloween Carnival at Del Amo Park . . . . Oct. 31, 1984
First Annual Christmas Can Drive and Teen Dance . . . . . . Dec. 21, 1984
8:00 p.m. to 12:00 a.m.

FOOTBALL BONANZA

During this Fall, we will be offering excursions to the local high school football games. (Banning and Carson). Space will be limited to the first 18 sign-ups. Tickets must be purchased on your own. All ages welcome.

Flash! A Special Bulletin! Anderson Park is on the lookout for volunteers with pizzazz, fun, outgoing attitude, motivation and last but not least, just plain downright, upright personalities. So if you fit any of the above qualifications. Don't Walk!! but run to Anderson Park. Call us at 639-0001 for more information. *Remember Anderson Park Needs You!! Volunteer Today!!*

SPECIAL EVENTS

Day at the Moto Cross............................ To Be Announced
Banning vs. Carson Dance........................ To Be Announced
Halloween Jubilee .... Oct. 30, 1984

AVALON PARK
700 East Gardena Boulevard - (213) 538-0019
Center Director - Jerome Haywood
Assistant Center Director - Shelley Randolph

HOURS OF OPERATION

Monday-Friday .... 3:00 p.m. - 9:00 p.m.
Saturday .... 10:00 a.m. - 5:00 p.m.
Sunday .... 12:00 Noon - 5:00 p.m.

CO-ED AEROBIC CONDITIONING

Aerobic conditioning is a complete physical fitness program. The class is offered to men and women on Tueday and Thursday from 7:00 p.m. to 8:00 p.m. and on Saturdays from 10:00 a.m. to 11:00 a.m. This program motivates exercise to help you stay fit.

UPCOMING SPECIAL

Tribute to Martin Luther King (Jan. 13, 1985 — 12:00 noon to 5:00 p.m.)

CALAS PARK
1000 E. 220th Street - (213) 518-3565
Center Director - Shannon Murphy

HOURS OF OPERATION

Monday-Friday .... 3:00 p.m. - 9:00 p.m.
Saturday .... 10:00 a.m. - 5:00 p.m.
Sunday .... 12:00 Noon - 5:00 p.m.

DRAMA CLUB

This club is designed for kids who want to participate in upcoming youth drama productions. Open to youths ages 8-13 years of age who want to learn all aspects of putting on a play.

CLINIC FOOTBALL & SOCCER

Calas Park is offering a football and soccer clinic for children 5 through 8 years of age. The children will learn the fundamentals of football and soccer and team sportsmanship. Please contact the park for specific dates and times.

CHILDRENS ACTIVITIES

We like to offer a broad variety of activities for participation by children. Such activities held every week are Arts & Crafts, Cooking, Safety Club, and Tiny Tots. Please contact park for specific day & times.

WOMEN'S CONDITIONING

This class will offer instruction in exercise and an all around fitness

Note. From City of Carson, California, Fall 1984, "Recreation Program" (newsletter), *13* (11), p. 24.

MAIL-IN — REGISTRATION FORM
Fill out all information — PLEASE PRINT

NAME: _____

ADDRESS: _____ CITY: _____ ZIP: _____

HOME PHONE: _____ WORK PHONE: _____

Name of Participant	Birth Date	Class Number	Name of Class	Class Fee	Office Use Only
			MUST SEND SEPARATE CHECK FOR EACH CLASS		

ALTERNATE CLASSES IF FIRST CHOICE IS FILLED

Name of Participant	Birth Date	Class Number	Name of Class	Class Fee	Office Use Only

REFUND POLICY

REFUND DEADLINE: March 30, 1984

Classes not reaching required minimum will be cancelled and fees refunded.

An administration fee of $2 will be deducted from all refunds requested by patrons.

Requests for refunds must be in writing and **accompanied by your cash register receipt for the class** and received by above refund date.

PLEASE REMEMBER TO ENCLOSE A STAMPED SELF-ADDRESSED ENVELOPE
MAKE CHECKS PAYABLE TO REDONDO BEACH REC & PARKS
RELEASE OF LIABILITY AND ACKNOWLEDGEMENT OF DEPT. REFUND POLICY

I absolve and agree to hold harmless the City of Redondo Beach. its employees. officers or agents from any liability which may result from my participation. or that of any minor in my legal custody, in the above activity; if the participant is a minor, I also give my permission for his/her participation in the above activities, and for any necessary emergency medical treatment.

SIGNATURE _____ DATE _____

Note. From Redondo Beach, California, Spring 1984, "Recreation Program and City Newsletter," p. 27.

    b.   The prescriptive approach, in which the activities provided are directed at achieving rather specific outcomes, primarily changes in a participant's recreation and other behaviors.

    c.   Therapeutic recreation services, which emphasizes rehabilitation, education, and counseling and recreation activities provided on a continuum from prescriptive to enabling services.

d. Special events—the promotion of activities for special occasions and a method of implementing and culminating activities, all of which are organized and directed by the organization.
2. Outreach and referral services.
   a. Outreach is a process for extending the leadership, activities, and services of an agency beyond its boundaries; mobile programs, roving leaders, transportation, and technical assistance to groups and other agencies are examples of outreach.
   b. Referral services are provided for individuals seeking additional recreation opportunities provided by an agency and other organizations. Educational and, in a therapeutic setting, leisure services enable people to enhance their capacity for participation.
3. Enabling services, which are all recreation services that lead to recreation activity. In this context, enabling services are provisions that permit individuals and groups to initiate recreation activities with a minimum of direction or intervention by an organization's personnel. Examples are:
   a. Opportunities for free or spontaneous activities occurring as a result of using recreation areas and facilities.
   b. Opportunities for the organization of special-interest groups, hobby groups, and club groups. The activities can range from pursuing common interests to social service projects with individuals and groups using recreation areas and facilities for organizational meetings and activities.

The continuum of activities that a programmer can plan, organize, and implement enables a system to provide a comprehensive program. Direct and enabling services are provided to enhance opportunities for all participants to enjoy recreation. These activities contribute to human growth and development and enrich the quality of life. Recreation programming is simply helping people enjoy recreation and leisure experiences.

SUMMARY

The first five phases of the systems approach to program planning enable the programmer to plan, organize, and develop a comprehensive array of recreation activities and leisure opportunities. The activities and opportunities are planned to enable people to engage in and enjoy recreation experiences that are related to their needs, interests, and desires. All the planning and preparation accomplished by a programmer will not enable people to enjoy recreation if the programmer does not initiate a method of informing and inviting people to participate in the planned program.

The programmer finalizes and implements plans to promote planned activities and begins the program in the sixth phase of the systems approach. Program promotion involves establishing an effective method of informing, inviting, persuading, and reminding a system's patrons about the opportunities being provided. Verbal, written, and visual messages are developed to inform and invite people to participate in recreation activities that have been developed to satisfy their needs, interests, and desires. The participants' needs and interests are considered in planning a program and in planning how to promote the program and other recreation activities. The programmer plans to get people's attention and effectively inform them about the activities planned. The promotional program is designed to enlist their participation.

To promote a program, a program planner may announce several times in a newspaper that an agency is sponsoring a program, arrange for several public service announcements on local radio and television, highlight the program in the program brochure, place posters in conspicuous places, and give handouts to people using a facility.

Personal contact is the most effective method of promoting a program; however, to effectively inform the greatest possible number of potential participants, the programmer relies on advertising, public relations, publicity, and program incentives to involve people in planned activities. The methods used to disseminate program information, like the activities planned, should be related to the participants' needs and abilities and stated in a manner so that the invitation is clearly understood.

Agencies providing self-sustaining programs are effectively using quarterly newsletters and program brochures to promote their activities. Generally, between four and six weeks is involved in promoting a program, regardless of the method used to promote it. Two additional weeks are allowed for registration and a one-week grace period allotted for completing final arrangements before a program is begun.

Recreation activities and leisure opportunities are planned as direct services, outreach programs, and enabling services. This continuum of service enables an agency to sustain a comprehensive program for its constituents by intitiating new and different activities at appropriate times during the program year, year in and year out.

ENDNOTES

1. Howard, D. R., & Crompton, J. L. (1980). *Financing, managing and marketing recreation and park resources,* (p. 448). Dubuque, IA: W. C. Brown Company.
2. Owen, J. L., Page, P. A., & Zimmerman, G. (1975). *Communications in organizations.* St. Paul, MN: West Publishing Co.
3. Howard and Crompton, p. 456.
4. Tillman, A. (1973). *The program book for recreation professionals,* (p. 70). Palo Alto, CA: National Press Books.

11

FEEDBACK AND EVALUATION

The final phase of the systems approach to recreation programming is feedback and evaluation. Feedback is an inherent characteristic of a system that provides the information used to control and regulate the program-planning process and the system's output. Evaluation is a continuous process of determining whether the specific objectives of an agency are being or were accomplished. The process involves assigning a value related to the level of accomplishment, effectiveness, or efficiency. Evaluation is directed at improving the system's operational effectiveness and the quality of the programs provided.

This chapter examines the use of feedback in the development of and for the evaluation of recreation programs. First, internal feedback, which is used to control and regulate the program-planning process, is examined. Internal feedback serves to focus the planning effort on the attainment of a system's goals and program objectives to produce activities related to the needs of a system's constituents. External feedback provides the information used to evaluate the system's overall effectiveness and efficiency in achieving its goals and objectives.

INTERNAL FEEDBACK

Internal feedback provides a continuous flow of information that is used for the formulative evaluation and the development of a recreation program. It is the feedback that occurs within and between the system's planning phases and between the subsystem component parts of a system. Feedback enables the programmer to concentrate on the development of activities that are consistent with the system's goals and objectives and responsive to people's needs. The system's goals provide general directions for planning recreation programs. Subsequently, feedback is used to compare the results of the sequential planning phases with the system's general purpose. In the second phase of the planning process, feedback is used to determine which needs and resources can be acted on and used to plan responsive activities. The decision to act on any given need or use any available resource is contingent upon feedback confirming that it is appropriate to proceed with the planning of a particular needs-related activity. Programmers consistently use feedback to compare the results of the planning process with the system's goals.

In the second phase of the planning process, the needs-assessment and resource-identification process produces external feedback. Needs and resource information is provided by the external feedback process. This is illustrated by Figure 11.1, which traces feedback through the first two phases of the systems approach to recreation programming.

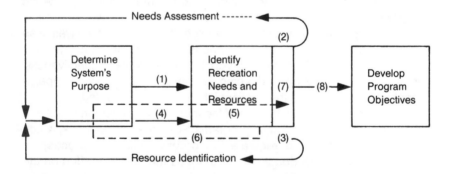

FIGURE 11.1 *Internal and external systems feedback.*

Number 1 represents the implementation of the needs-assessment and resource-identification phase. Numbers 2 and 3 represent needs assessment and resource identification, respectively. Number 4 represents feedback, the input of needs and resource data, and number 5 is the analysis of needs and resource data through number 6—the feedback that compares identified needs and resources with the system's goals. The decision to act on the needs that are found to be compatible with the system's purpose is represented by number 7 and the implementation of the program objectives phase is number 8. External feedback occurs as a result of the needs-assessment and resource-identification processes and internal feedback occurs as a result of comparing needs and resources with goals.

Internal feedback links the system's sequential planning phases into an interdependent and interrelated planning procedure and serves to control and regulate the systems approach to program planning throughout the entire process. In the process of developing program objectives, internal feedback confirms that the plans address people's needs and the system's purpose. In the activity analysis and cost-benefit analysis phase, the programmer uses program objectives as the criteria for determining which activities will be included in the system's general program. Feedback is used to assure the programmer that the plans developed through the first five phases of the planning process can be initiated. It verifies that the planned activities, programs, and services are compatible with the system's goals, program objectives, and the needs of the system's constituents through the promotion and implementation process.

Continued internal feedback within the planning phases and between the sequential phases serves to focus the planning effort on the attainment of a system's goals. The activities, programs, and services provided by the systems approach are planned to be compatible with the system's stated purpose and responsive to the needs and interests of the people that a system serves. Feedback provides the information used to compare planned results with actual results and it is the major source of information for evaluating the system's overall effectiveness and efficiency in achieving its purpose.

EXTERNAL FEEDBACK

External feedback occurs as a result of a system's output. It serves the programmer by providing information related to

1. Recreation needs and resources.
2. Confirmation of people's interest or disinterest in the planned and sponsored programs.
3. Evaluation of programs.
4. Identifying ways and means of improving program effectiveness and efficiency.

External feedback is generally spontaneous and normally based upon a subjective appraisal of a system's activities, programs, or services. Information received from spontaneous feedback is used for the informal evaluation of a recreation and leisure-service system. Programmers cannot discount these private and subjective evaluations because they serve the individuals who make them. Generally, on the basis of a subjective evaluation an individual will decide whether or not to participate in a planned activity or whether or not to support a planned program or the sponsoring agency. Therefore, he or she has a direct effect on the success or failure of a system's programming effort. Subjective evaluation of recreation and leisure services must be accounted for in the formal evaluation of a system's effectiveness and efficiency. This evaluation provides a source of information for developing the formal and objective instruments used for the operational and summative evaluations of a recreation program. Information for the formal evaluation of a program is collected through a controlled feedback process, which provides specific information related to the system's effectiveness and efficiency.

PROGRAM EVALUATION

System's feedback provides the information used for conducting four types of evaluation inherent in the systems approach to recreation program planning. The four types of evaluation are as follows:

1. Formulative, which is the measurement of the system's internal effectiveness and efficiency during the planning process.
2. Summative, a cumulative measurement of the results of providing activities, programs, and services which are normally reported in qualitative and quantitative terms.
3. Qualitative, which is a measurement of the relative value or worth of a program.
4. Quantitative, which is a measurement of program results normally reported in terms of numbers served or activities provided.

In fact, recreation programs are constantly evaluated by those who plan and conduct activities; by those who participate in activities; and by nonparticipants, administrators, and others. It is essential that the evaluation process be planned to be as objective as possible. Objectivity provides for the impartial collection, analysis, and interpretation of qualitative and quantitative evidence related to the system's effectiveness and efficiency in attaining its goals and program objectives.

According to Theobald,[1] evaluation concerns itself with making judgments about program results and it involves providing information related to the worth or value of a program. It consists of identifying reasons for program success or failure, discovering the principles underlying success and methods of increasing effectiveness, or redefining procedures for attaining objectives.

The formulative evaluation occurs while a program is being planned and serves to enhance the planning process and the development of relevant and responsive recreation activities for people. Nolan[2] suggested that evaluation involves three or more parties—the participant, programmers, and administrators—and proposed a systematic procedure for evaluating the three parts of a program. These parts are the evaluation of the "input or planning phase; the process, or period of time to which the program is run; and the outcome or results." The process or operational and summative evaluations of a program occur after program implementation. They involve participants, programmers, and administrators who cooperatively collect, analyze, and interpret data related to the attainment of a system's goals and objectives. Howe[3] suggests that "social research techniques, particularly for the collection, analysis and interpretation of information" are appropriate procedures for conducting the summative evaluation of a program.

The procedures used to evaluate recreation programs should allow for all parties to participate in the process, provide for the operational and summative evaluations of the program, and provide for the immediate analysis and interpretation of the evidence gathered. An effective procedure will provide for reliability and validity. Reliability refers to the accuracy or consistency of the evaluation and validity is an indication of whether a procedure measures what it is designed to measure.

Checklists provide one method of collecting operational and summative data for the evaluation of a recreation program. They provide one of the most time-efficient methods available and can be used for an objective and systematic evaluation of a system's programming effort, effectiveness, and efficiency. Theobald[4] explains that "efforts" are variables such as budget, staff, facilities, and equipment, and the effectiveness is measured in terms of the extent to which a system achieves its goals and objectives. Efficiency is the bridge between effort and effectiveness and refers to how resources are used to achieve results. It is a cost-benefit measurement in which the lower the cost in relation to the production of benefits, the greater the efficiency.

Programmers have a professional obligation to evaluate all aspects of a program and should determine how a program will be evaluated prior to implementation. The purpose of, subjects or topics of, procedures for, and criteria for the operational and summative evaluations should be determined during the operational planning phase. The procedure should allow for participants, programmers, administrators, and others to participate in the process and provide for the qualitative and quantitative analysis of data related to the system's effectiveness and efficiency in achieving its program objectives. The operational and summative evaluations of a program are a logical extension of the formulative evaluation and the procedure provides the programmer with a continuous assessment of the program-planning process. The formulative evaluation contributes to the development and implementation of relevant and responsive recreation activities for people.

The operational evaluation is an ongoing assessment of a program during its operation and it uses feedback from the registration process and activities to control and correct any discrepancies between planned and actual results. Feedback from the registration process generally provides the programmer with the first indication of whether a program is acceptable to the system's constituents. The operational feedback and evaluation process provides the programmer with a method of determining the following:

1. Is the program achieving anticipated results?
2. What aspects of the program are proceeding according to plan?
3. What aspects of the program are not proceeding according to plan, and why?
4. What, if anything, can be done to immediately improve the program?
5. Are the activities meeting the participants' needs and expectations?

The summative evaluation is the final phase of the evaluation process and the systems approach to recreation programming. It occurs at the end of a program and provides information for the comprehensive evaluation of the program-planning process, the program's operation, and the results or outcomes. The summative evaluation determines if a program achieved its objectives, if it was operated effectively, and if the activities had an effect or impact on the participants or the community at large.

Program evaluation serves two purposes. First, it provides information for improving a recreation program. Second, it provides a means of documenting qualitative and quantitative evidence that can be used to justify the programming effort. A systematic, effective evaluation of a program will use a system's goals and program objectives as the criteria for comparing observable and measureable results with planned outcomes. The systems programmer's ability to objectively evaluate is enhanced by the use of program objectives and information revealed about an activity by the activity-analysis procedure. Program objectives specify the activities, program format, target population, area, facilities, equipment, and materials that are used to conduct activities, the leader-instructor's responsibilities, and duration of a program. The activity analysis provides the programmer with greater insight into the purpose, content, procedures, outcomes, and behavioral characteristics inherent in an activity. The programmer can therefore develop a definitive idea of program results as the criteria for measuring a program's effectiveness and efficiency in attaining results.

To provide the actual criteria for evaluating program objectives, the elements of an activity must be translated into qualitative and quantitative standards. Theobald[1] has defined standards as "prescribed criteria of acceptable, desirable or optimal qualities or performance. They are usually established by concensus of expert opinion" or through extensive research. They are based upon rules, regulations, policies, procedures, and experiences, and are used to compare effort with results. The American Red Cross, for example, has established standards for the various levels of swimming competency. Beginners who successfully perform all the specified skills in a prescribed manner are advanced to the intermediate level and those who do not perform in the prescribed manner are retained in the beginners classification. The swimming standards established by the Red Cross describe in detail the minimum level of acceptable performance for each swimming classification.

The programmer will discover, when evaluating a recreation program, that often two or more sets of criteria are required to effectively evaluate—one for participants, another for the activity, and another for the leader or instructor. In swimming, for example, a swimmer will be evaluated on the basis of proficiency. A beginning swimmer must float for so many seconds in deep water and swim twenty-five yards to pass the test. The class evaluation will consist of comparing the total number enrolled with the number of students who successfully learn to swim after a specific number of lessons. The qualitative evaluation will compare swimming form, speed, and distance and the percentage of students who pass the course within a given time frame. Thus, there is a quantitative, qualitative, and performance evaluation inherent in one situation and the programmer has evaluated the individual swimmers, the class, and the instructor's ability to teach swimming.

A programmer may be responsible for developing local standards for qualitative and quantitative evaluation of a program. Standards can by systematically developed to describe desirable or acceptable behavior or performance, for other descriptive purposes, and as measures of quality and quantity. Performance standards based upon skill level, time, distance, accuracy, and achievement are used for qualitative purposes. Standards based on age, sex, and ability level are used for descriptive purposes. Standards related to numbers of participants, areas, facilities, equipment, programs, and leaders are used for quantitative purposes. In fact, standards have traditionally been used as the criteria for evaluating all aspects of a park and recreation organization's operations.

The programmer can use concisely defined standards as the criteria for measuring the factors and variables inherent in a recreation program and assign a related worth or value to a specific function or performance. The use of standards to describe levels of quality or quantity improves the objectively of the evaluation process. They especially enhance objectivity when checklist and other limited-response research techniques are used to observe or collect feedback about a particular program.

Considering that three or more parties may be involved in the formal evaluation of a program, it is advisable to use checklists or closed-end questionnaires to evaluate programs. Participants are requested to take a few moments to evaluate the program and then are given a checklist form to complete. Programmers will use checklists to observe programs during the operational phase; administrators will use participant responses and programmer's reports to evaluate program performance and compare results with other data to measure a program's impact on a community.

Program planning worksheets can be transformed into checklists or questionnaires and used for the formulative, operational, and summative evaluations of a program. Checklists provide a concise, convenient, and uniform instrument for collecting information for evaluating a program. They are easily administered and interpreted because they are limited in scope and depth. They can be modified to provide for a range of responses to specific questions or statements and to reveal information about program quality, quantity, effectiveness, and efficiency. Using a program-planning worksheet, a programmer can develop a series of questions or statements about the attainment of program, behavioral, or performance objectives that are related to the planning, implementation, operation, and impact of a program. Objective statements or questions about the following can be developed to collect information related to a system's effectiveness and efficiency.

1. Program organization and content.
2. Program personnel or leadership.
3. Areas and facilities (physical arrangements and maintenance).

4. Supplies, equipment, and materials.
5. Program format and scheduling.
6. Program promotion and publicity.
7. Registration procedures and program fees.
8. Emergency procedures and risk management.
9. Program implementation, operation, and results or impact.

Corresponding uniform qualitative and quantitative criteria can be developed to provide for appropriately evaluating each item. A five-point rating scale similar to the Likert attitudinal rating scale—strongly agree, agree, neutral, disagree, and strongly disagree—may be used to provide for a range of responses.

The checklist or questionnaire should be arranged so that directions for completing it are provided in block paragraph form at the top, the specific statements or questions are listed in categories on the left-hand side of the form, and five vertical columns are placed on the right-hand side for checking a corresponding response. Concisely defined standards or criteria for evaluating the level of achievement, performance, efficiency or effectiveness, and the quality or quantitative factors related to a program must be developed and specified for each column. The specific criteria used for the evaluation will be determined by the purpose of the evaluation; if it is designed to determine quality, qualitative responses are provided. If it is a comprehensive evaluation, different sections can be developed to assess quality, quantity, effectiveness, and efficiency.

In Redondo Beach, California, the Recreation and Parks Department annually sponsors a local Hershey's National Youth Track and Field Meet. Approximately 10 to 11 percent of the city's eligible youth participate in the meet, which is considered to be successful in spite of the low level of participation. The meet is a citywide special event that provides for limited age-group competition in track and field events, boys against boys and girls against girls. It serves to unite the community to provide the youth with an opportunity that ordinarily would not be provided by another organization. It has provided the many volunteers who conduct the events, officiate, tabulate results, and present the awards with as much pleasure and enjoyment as it has the participants. A review of the summative evaluation of the 1984 meet revealed that the committee made one major recommmentation—to reevaluate the registration form and make it less confusing. Otherwise, the general consensus of the community at large is to continue to sponsor the meet.

There are prevailing attitudes about recreation and park organizations and it is advisable to periodically use an attitudinal rating scale to assess constituents' attitudes about program offerings. The programmer, for the comprehensive evaluation, should include an attitudinal section in the total package. Separate forms should be developed to be used by participants, programmers, administrators, and others who will evaluate a program. The content of the forms should be similar to provide for the input of different perspectives into the process. Program evaluation is an extension and continuous process that enables a programmer to improve a program and to justify it.

Theobald,[1] Edginton and Williams,[5] and Farrell and Lundegren[6] have outlined procedures and explained several methods of evaluating. Farrell and Lundegren provide instructions for developing questionnaires, checklists, and attitudinal scales. It is strongly advised that a programmer consult one of the above references or others to design and construct an instrument for evaluating a program.

A systematic evaluation of a recreation program can be accomplished using a checklist or a closed-end questionnaire. This approach limits questions, statements, and responses to a carefully selected list of concisely stated objectives and a designated range of possible responses. The program process or operation, participants' performance, and the program impact can be evaluated using this type of form. It is recommended that a space for recording evaluator comments be provided for each category included on the checklist or questionnaire. This allows for special notations or extenuating circumstances that influence an evaluator's response to a particular item. Quantitative items should precede qualitative statements and attiitudinal summaries should be placed in the final section of the instrument.

Programmers are primarily concerned about program effectiveness and have used checklists to determine if participation

1. Exceeds anticipated results and additional activities should be provided.
2. Is balanced between actual and expected levels, and no changes or modifications are required to improve the quality or quantity of specific activities.
3. Falls below expected levels and modifications are required to improve effectiveness.

Operational decisions are made in relation to the evaluation of feedback using the above criteria. Gunn and Peterson[7] developed six basic questions that can be asked about program's effectiveness.

1. Were the group objectives appropriate to group goals?
2. Were the activities appropriate to the objectives?
3. Were the activities appropriate to the age and ability level of the group members?

4. Were the implementation strategies appropriate to group learning and development?
5. Were there unexpected outcomes?
6. Were the group objectives achieved?

Although these questions address group evaluation in therapeutic recreation settings, it is appropriate to ask the same questions about community and other recreation programs.

When developing or using a checklist-type evaluation, objective methods of observation or evaluation must be prescribed in the rules for assigning the same value to a given object by all raters or judges. Isaac suggests that "observer variance is at a minimum when precise criteria are defined."[8] A checklist using Gunn and Peterson's questions with a five-point summative rating scale is provided in Figure 11.2. The evaluator is asked to judge program effectiveness, rating effectiveness by marking an appropriate number on the one- to five-point scale. This illustration does not attempt to limit variance as it pertains to attitudes.

Legend: 1 - Strongly agree; 2 - Agree; 3 - Neutral; 4 - Disagree; 5 - Strongly disagree; NA - Does not apply						
	1	2	3	4	5	NA
1. Program objectives were appropriate.						
2. Activities were appropriate to objectives.						
3. Activities were appropriate to participant's age and abilities.						
4. Implementation strategies were appropriate.						
5. Group objectives were achieved.						
6. There were unexpected outcomes.						

FIGURE 11.2 *Program evaluation checklist (general evaluation).*

This brief example of a section of a program evaluation checklist, Figure 11.2, was presented to provide an illustration of a limited-response instrument. Additional sections for the purpose of evaluating program effectiveness and efficiency must be developed for program leadership, facilities, supplies, equipment, and other aspects of the program's operations, performance, and impact on the community and constituents. The programmer should approach evaluation with the same intensity and enthusiasm as program planning. The effective and efficient evaluation of a program serves to improve a system's and a programmer's ability to provide relevant and responsive recreation and leisure opportunities for people, individually and collectively. When this is accomplished, a system maintains program accountability. Theobald stated:

> There are a number of different models of program evaluation, many of which have been designed for specific fields of activity. It should be understood that evaluation models must be carefully chosen for their application and appropriateness to recreation and park programs, and often these models may require substantial modification in order to be effective.[9]

It is suggested that programmers adopt or develop a system to evaluate systems procedures, programs, and activities that serves their specific purposes. The procedure should be objective, reliable, and provide valid results.

The program evaluation process is not complete until the programmer, evaluator, or evaluation committee compiles, completes, and submits a report. Briefly, the report should specify the purpose of the evaluation, define what was evaluated, list the major questions and subquestions, and define the criteria used to evaluate. The methods or procedures for collecting the data should be explained in a separate section, and the major findings reported in another. A summary and recommendation should complete the report.

SUMMARY

Recreation programming is the process of identifying people's needs and organizing the resources necessary to produce activities that satisfy their needs and interests. The systems approach to program planning is a process that enables programmers to identify people's specific recreation needs and to use available resources to produce relevant and responsive activities. The planning process is facilitated by feedback, which serves to control and regulate the system's operations by focusing on the attainment of goals and specific objectives.

Feedback provides the system's programmer with a source of continuous information, which is used to compare the results of planning with the intentions of planning. Feedback provides the information used for the formulative, operational, and summative evaluations of a program.

Evaluation is a planned procedure for determining if specific goals and objectives have been achieved and if a program has had an effect on a delivery system's constituents. A system's goals and program objectives serve as the basic criteria used to compare results with intentions in any given situation. It is strongly recommended that programmers design and develop evaluation plans for their programs that can be used by participants, administrators, and others who will participate in the formal evaluation of a program. Evaluation is a continuous and extensive process that serves to improve program offerings and to justify their existence. The process should evolve from the formulative evaluation and continue through the summative evaluation, constantly providing for the objective analysis of a program's quality, effectiveness, and efficiency.

ENDNOTES

1.   Theobald, W. F. (1981). *Evaluation of recreation and park programs,* (p. 24). New York: John Wiley and Sons.
2.   Nolan, M. M. (December 1978). Evaluation of recreation programs. *Parks and Recreation, 13* (12), 40.
3.   Howe, C. L. Current strategies for evaluating leisure programs. *California Parks and Recreation,* 1982.
4.   Theobald, p. 23.
5.   Edginton, C. R., & Williams, J. G. (1978). *Productive management of leisure service organizations,* (pp. 232). New York: John Wiley and Sons.
6.   Farrell, P., & Lundegren, H. M. (1983). *The process of recreation programming, (2nd ed.,* pp. 206-247, 268). New York: John Wiley and Sons.
7.   Gunn, S. L., & Peterson, C. A. (1984). *Therapeutic recreation program design,* (p. 104). Englewood Cliffs, NJ: Prentice Hall, Inc.
8.   Isaac, S. (1976). *Handbook in research and evaluation,* (p. 100). San Diego, CA: Edits Publishers.
9.   Theobald, p. 102.

12

RECREATION PROGRAMMING

Recreation programming is a process of identifying recreation needs and organizing the resources necessary to produce activities for people, individually and collectively. The systems approach to recreation programming provides a framework for making appropriate decisions and accomplishing the following tasks. The systems approach enables programmers to:

1. Analyze an organization's (system's) purpose and use its goals and objectives as guidelines for planning programs.
2. Identify recreation needs and resources to enhance the planning of more relevant and responsive activities.
3. Use technical procedures to analyze needs, resources, activities, and costs to determine the most appropriate and feasible plan of action.
4. Plan, organize, promote, implement, and evaluate recreation activities.

The systems approach to recreation programming is an application of general systems theory, which can be used to analyze and explain operations and functions of any organization. The planning process enables recreation programmers to plan activities more effectively and efficiently.

Murphy proposed that "the primary objective of any recreation and leisure service agency, whether it be public, private or commercial, is to provide opportunities for people, individually and collectively, to enjoy leisure behavior."[1] This approach to planning can be used by all recreation and leisure-service agencies and any programmer to plan any program. Community (public and voluntary), therapeutic, and commercial recreation programmers use the systems approach to plan individual, group, and community activities. The analysis of all recreation and leisure-service agencies—public, voluntary, private, and commercial—reveals that they share a common purpose and serve a common constituency and resource base—the community. A community is a physical area that is inhabited by people who share a common identity by reason of their residence in a given area. Recreation and leisure-service agencies exist in, serve the people living in, and enhance the quality of life in a community. In turn, the community provides the financial resources required to operate all recreation and leisure-service agencies. Kraus and Curtis define community recreation as "those programs or opportunities presented by the community (either sponsored by government or by publicly supported voluntary agencies) which are designed to provide constructive and enjoyable leisure experiences for participants."[2] All recreation and leisure-service agencies operating within communities are organized and operate within the scope of local, state, and federal laws.

Traditionally, only tax-supported and voluntary agencies have been classified as community recreation services. Increased demand by all sectors of society, senior citizens, the handicapped, adults, and changing life-styles have served to expand and extend the scope of community recreation. Private and commercial agencies have capitalized on the demand for recreation opportunities and have become recognized providers of community recreation during the past twenty years, and will continue to provide many essential services for years to come. Contemporary economic conditions have limited support for public and voluntary recreation services during the past ten years in many sections of the country and public agencies in particular have altered their methods of operation. Voluntary organizations have also adopted new strategies to sustain their operations during this period.

Public agencies operated under the provisions of state park and recreation-enabling legislation and supported by local tax revenue have had financial limitations placed on their operations by inflation, tax-saving initiatives, and a realignment of public priorities. Public and voluntary organizations have initiated user fees and charges to sustain the delivery of many activities. Such voluntary organizations include the

YMCA, YWCA, the Boy and Girl Scouts, the Boys and Girls Clubs of America, and other agencies that are supported by the communities they serve. They sustain their services by charging membership fees, and rely on grants from fund-raising campaigns and soliciting gifts and donations from sponsors. Financial limitations have required public and voluntary organizations to revise their operations. They are now required to operate more effectively and efficiently in the 1980s than ever before in their histories.

Recreation areas and facilities owned and operated by individuals, associations, and corporations provide opportunities for their owners, members of the associations, and employees of corporations. These organizations are classified as private recreation when they provide services for their owners, members, or employees. Examples include operation of a swimming pool by a homeowners association, a country club, or an employee recreation association. Most private recreation and leisure-service agencies are operated on a non-profit basis.

Recreation services that are operated on a profit-making basis are classified as commercial recreation organizations. There is great diversity in the commercial recreation sector, which consists of large amusement parks such as Walt Disney World, Disneyland, and Six Flags parks; ski resorts; community health and fitness clubs; tennis and racquetball clubs; bowling lanes, and game rooms. The major difference among the individuals and organizations that provide recreation and leisure service is determined by their financial orientation.

Public, voluntary, and private agencies are primarily operated as nonprofit recreation and leisure services, while commercial agencies are profit making. Financial resources, tax revenue, and disposable income normally determine the scope of an agency's programs and facilities. In the 1980s the larger the agency, the greater the likelihood that some programs will be provided as governmental or social services, and others on a nonprofit basis.

THE ORGANIZATION OF RECREATION AND LEISURE SERVICES

The family-owned swimming pool is a private recreation facility used for the recreational enjoyment of family and friends. One member of the family assumes responsibility for the safe use of the pool and its maintenance. An adult generally supervises the pool when children are using it and there are strict rules for using the pool. The family provides for the operation, use, and maintenance of the pool in compliance with local building codes and zoning laws. With the exception of some maintenance services, the family is in complete control of the pool and common sense governs its use. When a family decides to operate a recreation facility as a commercial venture (and it has proven to be quite feasible for families to operate fishing ponds, campgrounds, and other recreation enterprises), it must assume a businesslike structure. One member of the family will be responsible for collecting fees, paying bills, and bookkeeping; another will provide for customer accommodations and activities; and others will take on other duties so that people can engage in recreation activities. The swimming pool and small family commercial venture illustrate that there is no need for a large organizational structure to provide recreation and leisure opportunities on a limited basis.

The operation of a voluntary youth sports association, the neighborhood Boy and Girl Scouts, and other recreation services requires a more elaborate organization to enable a greater number of people to benefit recreationally from the efforts of a few. Formal organizations, such as little league baseball, the Boy and Girl Scouts, and neighborhood service organizations, are administered by elected officials and appointed committees that cooperate to provide a number of recreation programs. In little league baseball, for example, one committee will be responsible for fund raising, another for grounds maintenance, and others will serve in individual capacities such as player agent, chief umpire, and coach and manager of the teams. The elected president and officials, including the board of directors, will collectively plan and organize the baseball program as a committee of volunteers.

The local Boy and Girl Scouts, the YMCA, YWCA, boys and girls club, police athletic league, and other nonprofit recreation agencies will employ one or more professionals to manage local programs. The scope of these programs is dependent upon the size and resources of a community, the physical and financial resources available, and the number and different types of facilities to be supervised and maintained. The larger the sponsoring agency, the more specialization in its operations.

The board of directors of a local family sports and fitness center will employ a general manager, a tennis pro, a fitness consultant, a head lifeguard, and pro shop and snack bar managers. Each employee will have general and specific responsibilities for planning and marketing recreation services. Local voluntary organizations will likewise employ an executive director and program directors for the physical, social, educational, cultural, service, and other programs. Public park and recreation will also employ a director, deputy directors, superintendents of parks, recreation, administrative assistants, supervisors, center and park directors, facility managers, program leaders, instructors, and specialists, along with park and staff personnel. The formal organization of an agency becomes more structured and individual positions become more specialized, the larger an organization becomes. There is a direct relationship between the number of programs provided and people served and the total resources used to support any agency, whether public, private, or commercial. Normally, the larger an agency's constituency, the more programs, services, and facilities it will provide. There are other factors that may serve to enlarge or limit an agency's recreation output. These include, but are not limited to, the philosophical beliefs of the community, agency board, commission, or other administrative authority; the political, social, and economic conditions; and constituent demand for programs and facilities.

Recreation and leisure-service agencies will generally employ one to four full-time professionals to plan, organize, and direct the activities provided at a specific facility. Public park and recreation departments in smaller cities often employ a small professional staff and contract with other organizations for the use of facilities and individuals to provide program leadership, instruction, and supervision for specific periods on a part-time basis. Other organizations that own their facilities will employ a director; supervisors of sports, cultural arts, therapeutic, senior citizen, and playground programs; and a number of recreation leaders.

In any situation in which people are provided an opportunity to engage in recreation activities, program planning is an inherent responsibility of individuals serving an administrative, supervisosry, and leadership position. Everyone in a leadership position, whether a playground or group leader, center director, facility manager, program coordinator, area or activity supervisor, or director of parks and recreation, must plan or contribute to the comprehensive program plans of an agency. Such planning may be limited to deciding when to schedule a directed activity or the sequence in which activities are conducted. An individual may be responsible for planning a sports, aquatic, arts, dance, or social program, or an agency's comprehensive program. This chapter will conclude with a discussion of how the systems approach to recreation programming can be used to plan community, therapeutic, and commercial recreation programs.

COMMUNITY RECREATION

Recreation and leisure-service agencies provide two types of community recreation programs—direct and enabling services, which can be classified as traditional or free programs, and self-sustaining programs. The systems approach to recreation programming can be used by an administrator, supervisor, center director, leader or recreation instructor, to plan either type of program.

· The systems approach requires the programmer to initially determine the sponsoring agency's purpose. Once this is accomplished, the programmer has a clear understanding of an agency's goals and objectives and can begin the needs-assessment and identification of resources process. When planning a traditional program, the programmer must identify specific problems, significant needs, and the community resources that can be used to sponsor free or governmental programs. Generally, public and voluntary agencies will sponsor free programs for participants who cannot provide recreation opportunities for themselves. The needs-assessment process can be used to identify constituents who have needs and interests and are willing to sustain special-interest activities. In planning community recreation programs, the needs-assessment process is used to identify constituents who are classified as

1. Dependent upon the agency to provide direct services, which are planned, organized, directed, and led by leadership personnel.
2. Semidependent upon the agency to provide them with assistance and special-interest programs, classes, and other organized activities conducted on a self-sustaining basis.
3. Semiindependent, who use the agency's areas and facilities to engage in self-directed activities.
4. Independent, who normally engage in recreation activities provided by another provider.

The programmer employed by a public agency will seek resources to organize responsive activities for all constituent groups and will plan a variety of direct, enabling, outreach, and self-sustaining activities.

Identifying the needs of an agency's constituents and the resources to support responsive activities enables the programmer to develop realistic program objectives. Program objectives should be related to people's needs and corresponding agency goals. They should be brief statements of program intent or purpose that can be defined in qualitative and quantitative terms and used as the criteria for program evaluation. General objectives must be developed for each program area—arts and crafts, outdoor, sports, and social recreation—and specific program objectives developed for each individual activity such as baseball, basketball, football, soccer, and tennis that is a component of the sports program.

The activity analysis and cost-benefit analysis are extremely important aspects of the process of planning community recreation activities.

The activity analysis enables programmers to conceptualize how constituents will behave while participating in an activity, and to anticipate potential problems. Knowledge of constituents' attitudes and projecting how they may react to various social and emotional situations inherent in an activity enables a programmer to plan and control program problems. The cost-benefit analysis procedure provides a method of determining if an activity can be adequately provided with available resources. These procedures enable community recreation programmers to make rational programming decisions.

The remaining systems planning processes for completing the operational planning, promotion, implementation, and program-evaluation phases facilitate the planning and delivery of a comprehensive community recreation program. Community recreation programmers who independently plan activities to be conducted by subordinate personnel should involve program leaders in planning discussions during staff meetings. Following the basic systems sequence enables an individual or a group of program planners to concentrate on the development of responsive activities.

THERAPEUTIC RECREATION

Planning activities for individuals with special needs—the ill, disabled, and handicapped—is generally the responsibility of a recreation therapist. The provisions of activities for people with special needs is called therapeutic recreation. The philosophical question of which term should precede the other is adequately discussed in the therapeutic recreation literature. Following common practice, program planning will be considered from the therapeutic recreation perspective. Jay Shivers suggests that "therapy is defined as anything that helps or aids recovery from an illness."[3] He suggests that recreation activity has a therapeutic value for all participants, because it may be any human endeavor pursued to satisfy an individual's social, physical, and emotional needs. It normally promotes a change in an individual's self-image and positive change can be considered to be the result of an encounter with a therapeutic agent.

Recreation activities provided for the physically, mentally, and developmentally disabled are generally planned to be enjoyable activities that promote a positive change in an individual's behavior or improve his or her functional abilities. Recreation activities are used when working with some special populations to reinforce prescribed behavior, to teach, and to promote socialization and normalization. Chubb and Chubb have defined therapeutic recreation as the "treatment of a person's physical or mental disability by medically supervised participation in recreation activity."[4] This definition limits therapeutic recreation services to medically prescribed activities and possibly to the hospital and institutional settings. Recreation activities pursued by the ill and disabled in any environment can be both therapeutic and recreational. It is difficult to distinguish between the use of recreation for therapeutic purposes and when recreation is pursued for its inherent values. Doctors of medicine and psychiatry can diagnose and describe treatments, including recreation activities, for individuals to aid in their recovery from an illness or injury; however, there are certain conditions that cannot be medically or surgically improved. There are congenital, disabling, and degenerative conditions that are beyond the present ability of medical science to correct. Recreation activities are provided for individuals and groups for whom there is no present medical means of alleviating a disabling condition; these activities are commonly referred to as therapeutic recreation services. Research reveals that recreation contributes to the rehabilitation, education, and recreation experiences of the

1. Developmentally disabled.
2. Emotionally or mentally ill.
3. Orthopedically or physically disabled.
4. Ill aged.
5. Socially maladjusted.
6. Sensory-impaired.
7. Neurologically or physiologically impaired.
8. Congenitally disabled.

Gunn and Peterson[5] developed a model for providing recreation services in hospitals, institutions, and the community. There are three phases in which recreation activities are utilized. The first is the rehabilitation phase, in which recreation activities are prescribed to assist in the diagnosis, adjustment, and treatment of an individual with a temporary or permanent disability or illness. The second is classified as the habilitation or educational phase, in which recreation is used to develop or maintain functional abilities. The third is the recreation phase, and recreation opportunities are provided for the enjoyment of the individual who may be hospitalized or institutionalized, or live in the community. The therapist is generally in control of the individual during the rehabilitation phase of the model; the habilitation phase is a transitional phase, and the participant (client) generally picks and chooses his or her own recreation activities in the recreational phase. The rehabilitation phase generally occurs in a hospital or institution and the other phases may occur in either a hospital, institution, or community environment. The "systems approach to therapeutic recreation program planning" developed by Peterson[6] is a planning tool for organizing individual and group activities for the ill and disabled. Peterson's planning process was developed for therapeutic recreation program planning and needs no modifications to effectively plan programs for the ill, disabled, and other populations with special recreation needs.

The systems approach to recreation programming presented in this text was developed to enable programmers to consider the recreation needs of the general population and to organize the resources required to promote feasible activities for community recreation purposes. The therapeutic recreation programmer will be required to modify the planning presented in this text. He or she plans with a clearly defined population to serve and a specific environment—the hospital, institution, or community—in which the activities will be provided. The specific purpose of the program and the needs, interests, and abilities of the individuals and groups served are generally limited by specific illnesses or disabilities. The planning of recreation activities for the ill, disabled, and other special populations requires that the sequential phases of the planning process be modified. Following the needs-assessment and resource-identification phase, the therapeutic recreation programmer should initiate the activity and cost-benefit-analysis phase rather than the program-objective phase. When developing a therapeutic recreation program, the activity-analysis process should precede the development of program objectives. This procedure allows the programmer to eliminate from consideration any activity in which a client would have difficulty performing or in which he or she would be physically or mentally unable to successfully engage. Therapeutic recreation services emphasize the positive effects of recreation experiences, and the systems approach to programming is used to identify situations in which specific activities will contribute to an effective rehabilitative, educational, or recreation program. Program objectives are developed to enhance the treatment, education, and recreation programs provided for special-population members served by the recreation therapist.

The systems approach to recreation programming is a method of planning that enables a programmer to utilize available resources to provide more need-responsive activities for individuals and groups of people. Programmers, when planning therapeutic recreation programs, modify the planning sequence as follows:

1. In phase one, the specific purpose of the program is determined, the population to be served is identified, and the program emphasis—rehabilitation, habilitation, or recreation—is specified.

2. In phase two, the programmer identifies the specific needs, interests, and abilities of the clients to determine the types of activities to be provided.

3. In phase three, various types of activities are analyzed to determine the specific requirements for successfully providing and adopting them to achieve specific therapeutic purposes and to satisfy clients' needs.

4. In phase four, program objectives are developed to specify the purpose of the program, the conditions in which they will be provided, and the anticipated results.

5. In phase five, the programmer completes the operational planning phase.

6. Phase six is the actual promotion, if necessary, and implementation of the program.

7. Systems feedback is continuously used to evaluate the program's effect and the participants' performance, and to facilitate the charting of an individual's or group's progress toward the achievement of specific therapeutic, educational, and recreational objectives. Feedback is also used to control the pace at which a program is conducted. For example, an ordinary child is expected to learn to swim within two to three weeks; a physically or developmentally disabled or sensory-impaired child, depending upon the severity of the disability, may require four to six weeks of intense instruction to reach to same level of proficiency. Feedback is used to control the actual delivery of the program's activities.

The systems approach to therapeutic recreation programming is a planning process that utilizes professional knowledge and analytical procedures to organize activities that contribute to a treatment program and enhance the general quality of life. It is a planning procedure that enables the programmer to develop a concept of what is to be accomplished; to analyze needs, and to plan, provide, evaluate, and justify recreation activities and programs for any population.

COMMERCIAL RECREATION

Commercial recreation can be defined as the provision of recreation opportunities, goods, and services by private enterprise for a profit. Samuels concluded from recent research that "commercial recreation and tourism-related enterprises. . . .will comprise the largest industry in the United States by the turn of the century."[7] The *U. S. News and World Report's* special reports on leisure spending in America estimated that people would spend in excess of $300 billion in 1985. Further analysis of recreation literature reveals that private and commercial recreation organizations provide both direct and indirect park, recreation, and leisure services. Direct services include opportunities to participate in neighborhood or wilderness recreation activities, while the indirect services provide support for recreation services ranging from transportation and living accommodations to financial services and retail outlets for goods and services.

In the public and voluntary sectors, recreation and leisure services are the primary function of the agencies; in the commercial sector, they may be a primary or secondary function of a business that is used to enhance customer relations. Most commercial recreation businesses are limited to one type of activity. Among the more prominent activities provided are bowling lanes; dance studios; ski areas; roller-skating rinks; health and fitness centers; and indoor tennis, racquetball, and handball facilities. Other facilities include amusement parks, theaters, and entertainment centers, and outdoor risk and adventure-type programs. According to Kelly,[8] all commercial recreation services are based upon the concept that people will pay for the recreation opportunities they want. These opportunities range from electronic games placed in the corner of a neighborhood convenience store to major amusement parks with comprehensive family vacation facilities. Americans have and are willing to spend their money in the pursuit of quality recreation experiences.

The systems approach to recreation programming can be used by commercial recreators as a basis for investigating the possibility of starting or expanding an existing recreation enterprise. Epperson[9] outlined a format for a feasibility study that consists of a market analysis, management analysis, and feasibility formula. With few exceptions, the initial investment of time, effort, and money in a commercial recreation enterprise involves a considerable risk of capital. A potential investor should seek advice from a small business consultant, lawyer, and financial analyst prior to investing money in any business. That person can use the systems approach to determine if a particular recreation service could be operated in a designated location and if it would be supported by the local community. The system's procedures can be used to conduct a market analysis; in fact, a market analysis and a needs assessment have similar functions. A market analysis, according to Epperson,[9] consists of

1. Goals and objectives of the enterprise.
2. Description of the services to be provided.
3. Description of the market—past, present, and future.

4. General characteristics of the market.
5. Location and accessibility.
6. Evaluation of community attitudes.
7. Attractiveness of the locality.
8. Availability of utilities.
9. Consideration of the competition.
10. Projected attendance.
11. Projected revenues.

Other factors to consider include local requirements for business licenses, zoning, and health, sanitation, and building codes in determining the feasibility of operating a recreation business.

The management analysis outlined by Epperson[9] consists of:

1. Initial or pre-opening expenses.
    a. Capital expenses.
    b. Equipment.
    c. Supplies.
    d. Advertisement and promotional expenses.
2. Operating expenses.

The feasibility analysis is an evaluation of projected income in relation to projected expenses. The detailed analysis and cash flow forecast required to secure a Small Business Administration loan is quite extensive and requires a good understanding of business practices, as well as a knowledge of recreation.

The systems approach to recreation programming can be used to explore the possibilities of expanding an existing commercial recreation services operation by following the prescribed procedures to obtain valid and reliable information to make an appropriate decision. The decision to provide a commercial recreation service is always based upon the projection that a profit can be realized.

SUMMARY

The systems approach to recreation programming is a planning process that can be used in any planning situation—public, private, or commercial. The planning process provides for the development of recreation activities that are responsive to the individual and collective needs of people and the sponsoring agency's goals. Effective program planning, whether for a community, therapeutic, or commercial recreation program, evolves from the identification and analysis of people's recreation needs, the formation of a need-related plan, and organization of the resources necessary to produce responsive activity opportunities. The systems approach to program planning is a socio-technical approach, social in that the agency-programmer interacts directly and indirectly with people to assess their needs and uses this information as the basis for planning activities. Technical procedures are used to analyze information during the needs-assessment and activity analysis-cost benefit analysis processes to ensure that the planned activities will accomplish specified objectives. A programmer's conceptual skills, professional training, and judgment are continuously called upon to make the decisions required to effectively organize the resources required to provide recreation activities.

The systems approach can be used to plan community, therapeutic, and commercial recreation programs and services.

ENDNOTES

1. Murphy, J. F. (1975). *Recreation and leisure services,* (p. 85). Dubuque, IA: W. C. Brown Company.
2. Kraus, R., & Curtis, J. (1973). *Creative administration in recreation and parks,* (p. 3). St. Louis: C. V. Mosby.
3. Shivers, J. S. (1981). *Leisure and recreation concepts: A critical analysis,* (p. 190-191). Boston: Allyn and Bacon.
4. Chubb, M., & Clubb, H. R. (1981). *One third of our time,* (p. 712). New York: John Wiley and Sons.
5. Gunn, S., & Peterson, C. A. (1978). *Therapeutic recreation program design,* (pp. 13-26). Englewood Cliffs, NJ: Prentice Hall, Inc.
6. Peterson, C. A. (1970). *A systems approach to therapeutic recreation program planning.* Unpublished doctorial dissertation, Columbia University, New York.
7. Samuels, J. B. (October 1984). Research update. In R. Kunstler (Ed.), *Parks and Recreation, 19* (10), 27.
8. Kelly, J. R. (1984). *Recreation business,* (p. 171). New York: John Wiley and Sons.
9. Epperson, A. (1977). *Private and commercial recreation,* (p. 22). New York: John Wiley and Sons.

APPENDIX

This appendix consists of a partial list of recreation activities provided by various agencies. This list was compiled by reviewing program literature, brochures, newsletters, and other material. The activities are listed in fifteen categories, which illustrates the diversity of contemporary recreation and leisure-service programs.

Arts and Crafts: Art is defined as the use of materials to create an object of esthetic value and crafts are objects created from materials that serve a useful purpose.

Basket weaving
Batik
Candle making
Ceramics
Collage
Coloring
Computer art
Copper enameling
Crocheting
Decoupage and
  Painting
  Graphics
  Banners

Junk crafts
Lapidary
Leather crafts
Macrame
Metal crafts
Model making
Mosaic
Needle craft
Papier-mache
Plastic crafts
Printing
Quilting
Rock painting

Cards
Murals
Paper models
Poster making
Printing
Sketching
Etching
Film making
Jewelry making

Sculpture
Sewing
Silk screening
Soap carving
Stained glass
String art
Tie Dyeing
Weaving
Wood crafts

Basic Movement: Movement is a new dimension in recreation programming; it is especially valuable in child care, rehabilitation, fitness, and exercise programs. The following activities promote movement, fitness, socialization, and conditioning.

Balancing activities
Climbing
Hopping
Jumping
Parachute games
Relaxation exercises

Rope jumping
Running
Skipping
Stretching
Throwing and catching
Turning and rotating

Dance:

Aerobic
Ballet
Ballroom
Creative/interpretive
Ethnic/folk

Modern
Round
Social
Square/western
Tap/clogg

Drama:

Community theater
Creative drama
Festivals
Mime
Musical comedy
Opera

Pageants
Pantomime
Plays
Puppetry
Story telling
Talent shows

A special note: In therapeutic recreation services, role playing and sociodrama have been used for rehabilitative, educational, and recreational purposes.

Education and literary activities:

Art classes
Astronomy

Foreign language study
Lecture series

Auto mechanics
Dance classes
Drama workshops

Ornithology
Sports clinics
Trips and tours

Games:

Board games
  Adi
  Backgammon
  Checkers
  Chess
  Chinese checkers
Box games
  Box hockey
  Foos ball (a table game)
  Skittles
Ball games
  Dodge ball
  Kick ball
Charades
Electronic games
Floor and lawn games
  Lawn bowling
  Floor hockey
  Putt-putt golf
Group games
  Four square
  Keep-a-way
Human checkers

Midnight
Party games
Horseshoes
New games
Paper and pencil
Running games
  Crows and cranes
Relays
  Tag games
Table games
  Billiards
  Bingo
  Card games
  Dutch shuffleboard
  Dominoes
  Pool
Table tennis
Target games
  Bean bags
  Darts
  Topple ball
  Shuffleboard

Hobbies and club activities:

Hobbies
  Collecting
    Antiques
    Art
    Buttons and pins
    Coins
    Dolls
    Gardening
    Guns
    Insects
    Models
    Painting

Clubs
  Art
  Badminton
  Boating and sailing
  Book
  Dance
  Drama
  Flying
  Gardening
  Glee
  Golf
  Hiking

Records
Sports cars
Repair/refinishing
Automobiles
Clocks
Furniture
Exhibitions
Judo
Pet shows

Judo
Model
Parachute
Rod and gun
Scuba
Ski
Sports cars
Table tennis
Tennis

Homemaking:

Cooking
Decorating
Fashion design
Home construction

Home remodeling/
  decorating
Lawn and garden care
Sewing and upholstery

Music:

Listening
  Classical
  Country and western
  Ethnic/folk
  Jazz
  Latin
  Popular
  Rock
  Soul
Playing/performing
  Band

Drum and bugle
Guitar
Orchestra
Piano
Singing/creating
  Chorus
  Concerts
  Composition
  Ensembles
  Glee club

Outdoor recreation:

Archery
Backpacking
Bicycling
Bird watching
Boating
Camping
Canoeing
Caving
Gardening
Fishing
Golf
Parachuting

Hang gliding
Hiking
Horseback riding
Ballooning
Hunting
Ice skating
Kayaking
Mountaineering
Nature study
Kite flying
Orienteering
Scuba diving

Rafting
Rappeling
Rock climbing
Rowing
Sailing

Skiing
Sledding/tobogganing
Sunbathing/swimming
Target shooting
Yachting

Physical fitness:

Baton twirling
Body building
Exercising and
   conditioning
Jogging and running

Roller skating
Slimnastics
Tumbling
Yoga
Walking

Social Recreation. Social interaction is inherent in many forms of recreation. There are a few exceptions, such as bird watching, reading, and listening to music. Social recreation denotes an emphasis on competition and places emphasis on congenial relations. Any activity involving cooperation, associations, membership, volunteer services, dating and courtship can be considered a form of social recreation. A few activities are listed.

Barbeques and
   cookouts
Club activities
   Adults
   Children
   Senior citizens
   Youth
Co-recreation activities

Dancing
Dating
Family outings
Parties
Picnics
Service activities
Visiting
Volunteering

Special events: Recreation activities that are promoted for special occasions—to celebrate a holiday, to begin or end a program, to recognize special achievements, to promote an agency's image, or to provide a change of pace—are considered to be special events.

Art shows
Awards banquets
Block parties
Citywide contests
Concerts
Dance recitals
Festivals

Holiday celebrations
Open houses
Parades
Special Olympics
Tournaments
Trips and outings
Winter carnivals

Sports and Athletics:

Archery
Badminton
Baseball
Basketball
Bobsledding
Bowling
Boxing
Cricket
Croquet
Cross country/marathons
Curling
Fencing
Football
Frisbee
Golf
Handball
Horse racing
Hockey, ice and field
Horseshoes
Judo
Karate
Lacrosse
Polo
Racing, automobile and boats
Boating

Racquetball
Rifle-pistol shooting
Rodeos
Rowing
Rugby
Sailing
Skating, ice and roller
Skateboarding
Soccer
Softball
Skiing, snow and water
Squash
Swimming and diving
Synchronized swimming
Tennis
Team handball
Paddle tennis
Deck tennis
Pickleball
Table tennis
Track and field
Volleyball
Water polo
Weightlifting
Wrestling

Vehicular Recreation:

Auto racing/cycle
  Drag racing
  Rallies
  Sprint cars
Bicycling
Boating
Canoeing
Kayaking
Motor boating
Rafting
Sailing

Rowboating
Campers
Motor homes
Trailers
Driving for pleasure
Flying for pleasure
Glider flying
Off-road vehicle use
Four-wheelers
Motor cross
Snowmobiling

INDEX